REGIONAL OUTLOOK
Southeast Asia
2009–2010

The **Institute of Southeast Asian Studies (ISEAS)** was established as an autonomous organization in 1968. It is a regional centre dedicated to the study of socio-political, security and economic trends and developments in Southeast Asia and its wider geostrategic and economic environment. The Institute's research programmes are the Regional Economic Studies (RES, including ASEAN and APEC), Regional Strategic and Political Studies (RSPS), and Regional Social and Cultural Studies (RSCS).

ISEAS Publishing, an established academic press, has issued almost 2,000 books and journals. It is the largest scholarly publisher of research about Southeast Asia from within the region. ISEAS Publishing works with many other academic and trade publishers and distributors to disseminate important research and analyses from and about Southeast Asia to the rest of the world.

REGIONAL OUTLOOK

Southeast Asia
2009–2010

ISEAS INSTITUTE OF SOUTHEAST ASIAN STUDIES

First published in Singapore in 2009 by
ISEAS Publishing
Institute of Southeast Asian Studies
30 Heng Mui Keng Terrace
Pasir Panjang Road
Singapore 119614

Internet e-mail: publish@iseas.edu.sg
World Wide Web: http://bookshop.iseas.edu.sg

The responsibility for facts and opinions expressed in this publication rests exclusively with the contributors and their interpretations do not necessarily reflect the views or the policy of the Institute, or its supporters.

ISEAS Library Cataloguing-in-Publication Data

Regional outlook: Southeast Asia.
   1998–1993–
   Annual
   1. Economic forecasting—Southeast Asia—Periodicals.
   2. Southeast Asia—Politics and government—Periodicals.
   3. Southeast Asia—Economic conditions—Periodicals.
DS501 S720   1992

ISSN 0218-3056
ISBN: 978-981-230-906-8 (soft cover)
ISBN: 981-981-230-907-5 (PDF)

Typeset by International Typesetters Pte Ltd
Printed in Singapore by Utopia Press Pte Ltd

CONTENTS

ECONOMIC OUTLOOK

PREFACE

Since its inception in 1992, the annual *Regional Outlook* series has offered readers concise and insightful analysis of political and economic trends in Southeast Asia and the wider Asia-Pacific region. Over the course of those sixteen years, *Regional Outlook* has tracked existing political and economic trends, identified new ones and assessed their implications for the Association of Southeast Asian Nations (ASEAN) and its member states. Written in an accessible and easily understood scholarly style, this publication is ideally suited for a modern audience of busy executives, professionals, diplomats, journalists and interested observers. The success of *Regional Outlook* is reflected in the loyal readership successfully built up over the years in Southeast Asia and beyond.

The year 2008 was a landmark year for ASEAN and its commitment to create an ASEAN Community by 2015. Most significantly, the ASEAN Charter was set to come into force in December after Thailand delivered the tenth and final instrument of ratification in November. The Charter will have far-ranging political, economic and social implications in that ASEAN will increasingly become a rules-based organization with its own legal identity. ASEAN's dynamic new Secretary-General, Dr Surin Pitsuwan, has already made good progress in turning the Association's aspirations into reality. In the aftermath of Cyclone Nargis, which devastated large parts of Myanmar, Dr Pitsuwan's unstinting efforts ensured humanitarian relief began reaching cyclone victims, underscoring how ASEAN can be an effective tool in times of crisis. On the domestic front, however, several ASEAN countries had to contend with political instability in 2008, especially Thailand, Malaysia and the Philippines. Political violence continued in southern Thailand, albeit on a reduced scale, while the failure of an agreement between the Arroyo government and the Moro Islamic Liberation Front was a major blow to peace-building efforts in the Philippines. Unfortunately political instability will continue to challenge several ASEAN members in 2009–2010.

On the economic front, growth will be lower for Southeast Asia in 2009 compared to previous years as a direct consequence of the financial crisis which began in the United States in 2007, worsened considerably in 2008 and then infected the entire global financial system. Even emerging economies have not been spared. Whether the impact of the slowdown of the U.S. and Japanese economies on ASEAN will be mitigated by demand from China and India is now questionable, as both economies are forecast to slow in 2009. Oil and commodity prices fell in the latter part of 2008 and this will ease inflationary pressures in Southeast Asia in 2009. But falling consumer demand in the United States and Japan does not bode well for the region given its dependence on both markets for economic growth. However, barring protectionist measures and future unexpected financial shocks which would further erode global economic confidence, it is expected that the world will ride out the current turmoil in about one to two year's time. Fortunately, leaders at the G-20 and APEC summits in 2008 stressed the importance of maintaining trade openness in the current economic slowdown. Economic integration will continue in the region, especially as the ASEAN Charter enters into force, though the pace may be slightly slower because of the global slowdown.

Regional Outlook 2009–2010 was written by a team of experts from within ISEAS and outside and in this edition several new writers were invited to offer fresh perspectives on future developments in the region. I wish to thank the editors, Ian Storey and Lee Poh Onn, as well as all the writers, for their valuable contributions.

K. Kesavapany
Director
Institute of Southeast Asian Studies

3 December 2008

INTRODUCTION

T wo events in the first month of 2008 symbolized the passing of one era in Southeast Asia's political development and the dawning of a new one. On 27 January, former Indonesian President Soeharto died at the age of eighty-six after a long illness. Perhaps more than any other Southeast Asian leader, Soeharto embodied a bygone age. The archetypal strongman had risen to power on the back of an attempted coup by the Indonesian Communist Party on 30 September 1965; at the time, nearby Indochina was wracked by conflict and Southeast Asia itself was riven by Cold War rivalries among the Great Powers. Soeharto ruled Indonesia for thirty-two years, crushing all political opposition but transforming the economic fortunes of the country. His passing was appropriately mourned in Indonesia, though in a country that has transformed itself into a vibrant democracy since the collapse of the New Order in 1998, few looked back with nostalgia at the former strongman's tenure.

Earlier in January, a political transformation of a different kind was taking shape. On the first day of the New Year, Dr Surin Pitsuwan assumed the office of Secretary-General of the Association of Southeast Asian Nations (ASEAN). As he took up his responsibilities, the dynamic former Thai foreign minister did not mince his words, warning that if ASEAN did not reinvent itself it risked marginalization and irrelevance: "Without a strong centre, ASEAN cannot remain the fulcrum of power plays in the region. It cannot remain in the driver's seat in political, economic and security affairs." In order to sit behind that wheel, ASEAN believes it needs a new license, and that new license is the ASEAN Charter. Signed in November 2007 during the Association's 40th anniversary year, the Charter introduces a rules-based framework designed to realize the aspiration of an ASEAN Community by 2015. During 2008, each of the ten members ratified the Charter, despite opposition by some parliamentarians in Indonesia who were concerned at the efficacy of the Charter, and politicians in the Philippines who argued that ratification should be linked to improvements in Myanmar's human rights situation. The stage seemed set for a new phase in ASEAN's development.

Regional crises quickly tested ASEAN's mettle, with mixed results. In early May, Cyclone Nargis barreled into southern Myanmar, killing more than 100,000 people and leaving millions more homeless. Myanmar's ruling generals had failed to give their subjects adequate warning of the impending catastrophe, and their unwillingness to admit foreign aid workers to help pick up the pieces angered and perplexed the international community. Recognizing that its credibility was on the line, ASEAN stepped in and persuaded the generals to cooperate with foreign donors. The Secretary-General's intervention ensured that outside humanitarian assistance began reaching the victims of the cyclone. ASEAN was deemed to have acquitted itself well.

The second test came in July when tensions erupted on the Thai-Cambodian border over land adjacent to the 11th century cliff-top Hindu temple of Preah Vihear. The flare-up occurred after Thailand's foreign minister had backed Cambodia's bid to designate the temple a UNESCO world heritage site. Thailand's Constitutional Court subsequently ruled the foreign minister's action as unconstitutional, leading both sides to beef up their military forces near the temple. ASEAN's offer to mediate was rejected by Thailand which felt the problem should be resolved bilaterally; Cambodia reacted by threatening to take the issue to the United Nations Security Council. An interim agreement to refer the problem to a joint border commission was hammered out, but tensions flared again in October when a gun battle between Thai and Cambodian forces broke out, leaving several soldiers dead on both sides. The incident not only underscored persistent and deep-rooted suspicions among the ASEAN members, but also the long distance still to travel before the Association could truthfully declare itself a security community free from the prospect of military confrontation.

Political instability was manifest in other parts of Southeast Asia in 2008, most notably in Malaysia, Thailand and the Philippines, three core members of ASEAN. In Malaysia, elections in March dealt a body blow to the ruling Barisan Nasional (BN) coalition, and especially to the dominant party, the United Malays National Organization (UMNO). For the first time in almost four decades, BN lost its two-thirds majority in the federal parliament, as well as control of five states. The devastating result sealed the political fate of Prime Minister Abdullah Badawi, who subsequently agreed to step down in March 2009 in favour of his deputy Najib Razak. Meanwhile, waiting in the wings was the former deputy prime minister, Anwar Ibrahim, now formal leader of the Malaysian opposition. The deadline he set for the downfall of the BN government through parliamentary defections — 16 September — passed without incident. However, since his re-election to parliament in August, Anwar had quickly established himself as a political force to be reckoned with. In the Philippines, the perceived illegitimacy of the administration of Gloria Macapagal Arroyo, and the weakness of state institutions, resulted in continued and pervasive disillusionment.

Events in Thailand in 2008 took a more worrying and violent turn. The December 2007 elections failed to restore political stability to the country after the ouster of former Prime Minister Thaksin Shinawatra in September 2006 and sixteen months of military rule. The People's Power Party (PPP) — a reincarnation of Thaksin's dissolved political vehicle Thai Rak Thai — won the election and its leader, veteran politician Samak Sundarajev, was appointed premier at the end of January. His appointment sparked demonstrations from the anti-Thaksin People's Alliance for Democracy (PAD) who accused Samak of being a proxy of the ousted prime minister. In August the PAD occupied government buildings in an attempt to force Samak to resign; Samak did resign on 9 September, but only after the Constitutional Court had found him guilty of illegally accepting payments for appearing on a TV cooking show. The PPP replaced Samak with Somchai Wongsawat,

Thaksin's brother-in-law. Violent clashes between the PAD and the police erupted in October, resulting in several deaths. Tensions escalated in November when the PAD laid siege to Bangkok's two main airports, crippling the country's lucrative tourism industry. The occupation ended on 2 December when Prime Minister Somchai resigned after the Constitutional Court dissolved the PPP for electoral fraud. The judgement will do little to resolve the underlying issues that have polarized Thai society.

On the perennial problem of ethnic insurgencies in Southeast Asia, 2008 brought more bad news. The daily catalogue of bombings, shootings and arson attacks continued in Thailand's Muslim-majority southern provinces, raising the body count above 3,700 since January 2004. With the Thai elite preoccupied by the ongoing crisis in Bangkok, the need for a political solution to the problem slipped further down the list of national priorities. In the Philippines, there were cautious grounds for optimism in the first half of the year that a peace deal to end the decades old insurgency in Mindanao was within sight. The government and Moro Islamic Liberation Front (MILF) reached a Memorandum of Agreement (MOA) to create an autonomous homeland in Mindanao, which finally settled the contentious issue of ancestral homelands. However, this optimism was crushed in August with the Supreme Court's ruling that the MOA was unconstitutional. Breakaway factions of the MILF vented their anger by launching attacks against the Philippine armed forces, leaving many dead and displacing more than 120,000 people. The MOA was rendered a dead letter.

As the authors in the Political Outlook section conclude, political instability in Southeast Asia in 2008 is likely to bleed into 2009 and beyond. This is particularly true in Thailand, where further clashes between the PAD and Thaksin loyalists could provoke the armed forces to intervene, setting off a fresh round of political crises. In Malaysia, the focus will be on UMNO's attempts to restore its political legitimacy while trying to fend off an energized opposition under Anwar Ibrahim.

Several countries will conduct, or prepare for, major political events in 2009–2010. Indonesia will hold parliamentary elections in

April, followed by a presidential poll in July. Whatever the results, all signs point to a peaceful electoral process that will further consolidate democracy in Southeast Asia's most populous country. The picture is less rosy in the Philippines, where political maneuvering in the run-up to the 2010 elections could lead to violence. In Vietnam, the ruling communist party will hold a mid-term plenary in early 2009, possibly resulting in leadership changes before the landmark 11th Party Congress in 2011.

Domestic politics aside, Southeast Asia's leaders will be watching with keen interest how the policies of U.S. President Barack Obama impinge upon the region. Given the strong fundamentals in U.S.-ASEAN relations, and Obama's stronger commitment to multilateralism than his immediate predecessor, the outlook for U.S.-ASEAN ties in 2009 is bright.

Dramatic changes in the economic climate in 2008 were beyond anyone's imagination. Warning signs were already present in August 2007 when the subprime mortgage crisis first surfaced, but the scale of the financial crisis that unfolded in 2008 caught everyone by surprise. By the end of the year many economies had already slipped into recession, with more expected to follow suit in 2009. Recovery may occur as early as 2010, but it is unlikely to be a speedy recovery. Financial conditions are likely to remain very difficult for the foreseeable future though one bright note is that inflation looks set to ease in 2009. The price of oil fell significantly in late 2008 and is expected to remain at current levels in 2009, bringing some relief to the economies of Southeast Asia.

The slowdown in the developed economies of the United States, the European Union (EU) and Japan during 2008 will affect the growth trajectory of Southeast Asian economies during the period 2009–2010. By early December 2008, the Euro-zone countries, the United States and Japan were all in recession. As a result, economic growth rates will be much slower in Asia: some economies will have growth rates that thread close to zero, while some will have double digit growth rates reduced to single digits. Emerging economies are expected to provide a source of resilience in this period of global downturn. Eventually, however, this cannot be expected to continue if major economies do not recover in the latter part of 2009–2010.

In the two years ahead, the growth forecast will remain positive for Brunei Darussalam with rates, however, expected to be below the 2 per cent mark. Lower oil prices do not bode well for the Bruneian economy though its diversification efforts will help to bolster its growth rates during this period of global downturn.

Growth in Cambodia has been nothing short of spectacular in the past few years but this is not expected to continue in 2009–2010: dollarization has limited the capacity of monetary authorities to mop up excess liquidity associated with the asset price boom, and handicapped the implementation of anti-inflationary measures. In a dollarized economy, inflows of capital in the form of dollars automatically increase the money supply, and the capacity of monetary authorities to do anything about it is limited. Rampant corruption remains a major problem in Cambodia requiring urgent attention.

The Indonesian stock market experienced a significant decline in 2008 and uncertainties are expected to last through 2009. The country's export and import sectors will be badly hit during 2009, due to reduced growth among Indonesia's main trading partners and volatile commodity prices. Liquidity constraints and the high cost of financing will be the major challenge facing the domestic economy in 2009. The performance of the economy in 2009 and 2010 depends on a well-functioning financial market, successful elections and the beginnings of a global economic recovery.

In Laos, economic growth is predicted to continue despite the global financial turmoil. The rate of growth will likely be about 8 per cent during 2009–2010, mainly due to the construction of new hydropower and mining projects, and commodity exports. Laos' industrial sector is forecast to continue to grow at double digits. Both the agriculture and service sectors will grow; the former due to increases in foreign direct investment (FDI) and the latter due to an increase in tourism and trade expansion.

Malaysia's banks are well capitalized and have little exposure to the toxic assets responsible for the global crisis. However, as it is export dependent, its growth prospects will also be negatively affected during this period of downturn. Malaysia's economy should be able to withstand a world recession in 2009, provided that global interest rates continue to decline. In Myanmar, owing to the lack of a conducive business environment, such as increasing government intervention, frequent changes in economic policies, restrictions in foreign trade sectors, private sector controls and the absence of a "level-playing field", growth prospects will continue to be low.

Like its neighbours, the Philippine economy will not be immune from the adverse impact of the global financial crisis. The increasing interdependence of the Philippines with the rest of the world, as seen in the openness of its trade and investment regimes, and increased reliance on international markets, will negatively affect its growth prospects. The same is even truer of Singapore which is the most trade-dependent economy in Southeast Asia. Singapore's growth prospects during 2009–2010 are at risk to due to its considerable linkages to the global economy, especially in areas such as finance and shipping. Nevertheless, the economy has some strong shock absorbers in place: the city-state has significant foreign exchange reserves, banks are well-capitalized and the corporate sector outside of property developers has been conservatively managed resulting in strong balance sheets. Large infrastructural projects, notably the integrated resorts, will also help to shore up growth during the forecast period.

Thailand's economy is forecast to grow at a slower pace in 2009 and 2010 due to decelerated exports and sluggish public investments. The uncertain domestic political situation, budget disbursement, global economic downturn and fluctuating oil prices will hurt the Thai economy during 2009–2010. However, the country's economic fundamentals remain satisfactory with declining inflation, manageable public debt level and ample international reserves.

For Vietnam, economic growth is likely to slow in 2009–2010. FDI inflows and portfolio investment is expected to fall and foreign exchange earnings from exports will also grow more modestly than in previous years. The domestic corporate and banking sectors will struggle in a less benign economic environment, having become bloated in recent years of rapid growth. Getting the corporate sector on a firmer footing will be a policy priority in 2009–2010.

In sum, Southeast Asia in 2009–2010 faces a host of political and economic challenges that will require a coherent response both from ASEAN as an organization and from the individual member countries.

Ian J. Storey
Lee Poh Onn
Editors

3 December 2008

POLITICAL
OUTLOOK

SOUTHEAST ASIA'S SECURITY OUTLOOK

By Tim Huxley

Southeast Asia's security outlook for 2009–2010 is not altogether positive. Instability in the domestic politics of several Southeast Asian states will persist, and the possibility of violence on the streets of some regional capitals cannot be ruled out. Hardship amongst ordinary people as a result of the global economic crisis may exacerbate existing political tensions while generating new ones.

In Thailand clashes between security forces and anti-government demonstrators had already led to one death in October 2008. Tension between the government of Prime Minister Somchai Wongsawat and the opposition led by the People's Alliance for Democracy (PAD) could lead to a new intervention in politics by the army in 2009. However, another coup will not resolve deep-seated antagonism between the populist forces aligned with former Prime Minister Thaksin Shinawatra and represented by Somchai's government and the agglomeration of liberal, middle-class elite and royalist interests in the PAD. In sum, Thailand's domestic disarray will persist through 2009.

In Malaysia, the parliamentary opposition has threatened a vote of no-confidence in the government as soon as it calculates that it has sufficient support through defections from the governing coalition. Such a vote might bring down the government, necessitating a transfer of power to the Pakatan Rakyat coalition led by Anwar Ibrahim. However, the Barisan Nasional government could try to retain power by declaring a State of Emergency pending new elections. Other possibilities include more extensive use of the Internal Security Act to detain opposition figures and accelerated moves to try Anwar on sodomy charges. Assuming the government survives, however, Abdullah Badawi's resignation as UMNO President and Prime Minister in March 2009, and his anticipated replacement by Deputy Prime Minister Najib Tun Razak, could reduce political tensions temporarily. One way or another, though, Malaysia's protracted political crisis will continue.

Elsewhere in Southeast Asia, the military regime in Myanmar will remain on unhappy terms with the people of the country, and economic problems may fuel new eruptions of popular discontent. In the Philippines, President Gloria Macapagal Arroyo will remain unpopular, but efforts in the Congress to impeach her will prove ineffective. In Indonesia, parliamentary elections in April, followed by presidential polls in July, will be largely peaceful. Exuberant rallies could lead to street clashes between rival parties, but there is every reason to think that the 2009 elections will highlight Indonesia's transformation from a violent and chaotic state apparently on the brink of disintegration at the beginning of this decade into a successful and highly stable decentralized transitional democracy.

Armed insurgency will continue to take many lives and undermine the stability of Thailand's three southernmost provinces. The Thai government and military, preoccupied with domestic political issues, are unlikely to give the southern crisis sufficient attention to make a negotiated settlement possible. The danger will remain that the Muslim insurgent groups could take their violent campaign to Thailand's capital and tourist resorts. In the southern Philippines, the Abu Sayyaf Group (ASG) will remain a serious threat in the Sulu archipelago, taking hostages for ransom and engaging in clashes with the Armed Forces of the Philippines. Since the breakdown of negotiations during 2008, significant elements of the Moro Islamic Liberation Front (MILF) have resumed their own insurgency on Mindanao, and major conflict there may continue into 2009. In diverse parts of the Philippines, the communist New People's Army will continue to pose a threat.

Terrorism will continue to fade as a threat in the region, as Indonesia's security forces continue to mop up remnants of Jemaah Islamiyah (JI) on Java and in other provinces. The execution in November 2008 of JI terrorists responsible for the 2002 Bali bombings may lead to demonstrations but will not significantly boost the JI cause. JI elements in the southern Philippines, sheltered by the ASG and MILF, will be mainly incapable of mounting significant attacks. Piracy, widely seen as a major regional security issue earlier in the decade, will also make little impact, though occasional attacks on merchant vessels will continue.

The strong domestic orientation of most Southeast Asian governments during 2009–2010, particularly as they cope with difficult economic circumstances, will undermine their ability to focus on regional and international issues. One consequence may be poor and unstable bilateral relations between some states in the region. Thailand and Cambodia will remain at loggerheads over their border dispute, with sporadic armed clashes perhaps becoming routine. Political upheaval in Malaysia could exacerbate bilateral points of tension with neighbours. In Malaysia-Singapore relations, conflicting claims over maritime features near the Pedra Branca lighthouse will remain a source of disagreement. Bilateral tensions and suspicions will remain an important motive for Southeast Asian states' military modernization programmes, though new restrictions on defence budgets resulting from the financial crisis may in some cases slow down these efforts.

The Association of Southeast Asian Nations (ASEAN) will continue its efforts to develop a political-security community while attempting to inject life into the wider regional bodies with a security ambit that it sponsors, including the ASEAN Regional Forum (ARF) and the East Asian Summit (EAS). However, ASEAN's widely-noted weakness in responding to Myanmar's crises in 2007–2008 and to the Thai-Cambodian dispute during 2008 means that it will face an uphill struggle to repair its tarnished image and restore the confidence of its members. Meanwhile, Australian Prime Minister Kevin Rudd's proposal in 2008 for a pan-regional Asia-Pacific Community has challenged the role of the ARF, which is widely seen as ineffectual. A fundamental reshaping of the regional security architecture may be under way. This could see, amongst other things, the ARF focusing increasingly on coordinating regional responses to human security threats such as natural disasters and pandemic disease.

A major rationale for reviewing regional security structures is that the power dynamics of Southeast Asia and the broader Asia Pacific are changing as China's power and confidence increase and as economic problems and political fallout from the Iraq war challenge the United States' capacity to assert itself internationally. Beijing will continue efforts to build multifaceted relations with Southeast Asian states. However, China's attempts to increase its long-term energy security will increasingly impinge on the interests of Southeast Asian states with claims in the disputed Spratly Islands, and could prove counterproductive if they seek to guarantee their security by maintaining or intensifying security relations with the United States. Moreover, the incoming U.S. administration in early 2009 is likely to energize Washington's diplomacy and engagement in multilateral structures in the Asia Pacific, a development which Southeast Asian governments will mainly see in a positive light.

ASEAN: NEW CHARTER, NEW OPTIMISM
By Rodolfo C. Severino

In seeking to discern what is in store for the Association of Southeast Asian Nations (ASEAN), it would be illuminating to examine whether the organization's new Charter will serve the Association well in the coming year and beyond.

The first question to ask is why ASEAN needs a charter at all. For forty years ASEAN scored some considerable achievements without a formal constitutive document. It relied instead on informal processes and personal relationships to arrive at common positions on critical international issues and matters that called for intra-ASEAN cooperation, such as trade, economic regionalism, contagious diseases, trans-boundary pollution and transnational crime. Without a formal charter, the Southeast Asian nations as a group have succeeded in getting other countries, including the Great Powers, to engage with Southeast Asia in friendly and constructive ways.

Yet, in November 2007, the ASEAN leaders signed the ASEAN Charter. Why? The political rhetoric aside, a number of objectives are apparent:

- To codify and regularize ASEAN's practices and symbols as they have evolved over the years;
- To make clear ASEAN's goal of becoming a "single market and production base";
- To adopt behavourial norms not only for inter-state relations, but also for states to adhere to in the relationship with their own people;
- To place squarely on 'ASEAN's leaders the responsibility for resolving issues on which consensus cannot be reached at lower levels; and
- To modify ASEAN's structures and processes so as to streamline and hasten decisions.

Ultimately, the Charter is supposed to enable ASEAN to integrate the regional economy more effectively and expeditiously, serve as a force for regional peace and stability and cooperate in dealing with common regional problems. In doing so, ASEAN should be better able to help people in Southeast Asia improve their lives.

This raises another question: will the Charter serve the purposes for which it was adopted? Put another way, how good a charter is it?

ASEAN: NEW CHARTER, NEW OPTIMISM (continued)

In seeking to answer this question, it is important to bear in mind that the Charter is the product of inter-governmental negotiations and that, like other international agreements, it is based on compromises designed to accommodate divergent positions, which often result from differences in national interests. Nevertheless, the Charter contains significant features that, if complied with, could help make ASEAN more effective. For the first time, ASEAN has adopted norms not only for inter-state conduct — to which the ASEAN countries have long adhered — but also for the internal behaviour of states: norms like democracy, human rights and fundamental freedoms, constitutional government, rule of law, social justice and good governance, with the stated intention of establishing a regional human rights body. While the Charter does not provide for a regional court, much less for a common military or other enforcement mechanisms, it does enshrine these norms and embodies ASEAN's commitment to them. The Charter thus gives governments and the people they represent something to invoke in case of egregious violations of these norms.

Before the Charter's adoption, the member states had, over the years, made commitments towards the achievement of certain regional goals. They had, for example, agreed on measures for creating a single market and production base in Southeast Asia. They had collectively adopted a "zero-burning" policy to prevent trans-boundary haze pollution. They had committed themselves to promoting and facilitating tourism in the region. And now they are adopting norms for the conduct of member states towards their own people.

The Charter puts in place measures to promote observance of these ASEAN commitments and to cultivate a culture of compliance. Some of these measures entail monitoring and reporting; others call for the establishment or strengthening of dispute-settlement mechanisms.

In case consensus on significant issues cannot be reached at the ministerial or officials' level, the Charter provides that national leaders have the responsibility for resolving the impasse. It does not specify that the leaders should resort to voting on the matter, but neither does it rule out that modality.

The Charter institutes certain changes to ASEAN's structures and processes that are intended to make decision making more expeditious. One of them is the creation of a Committee of Permanent Representatives stationed in Jakarta that would assume the decision-making functions of the ASEAN Standing Committee. The home-based ASEAN Directors-General, who used to constitute the Standing Committee, would take care of coordinating and promoting national compliance with ASEAN commitments and cultivating knowledge of ASEAN among their respective peoples.

The Charter legally enters into force thirty days after the deposit of the tenth instrument of ratification. The Charter goes into force on 14 December 2008, Thailand having deposited with the Secretary-General the tenth and last instrument of ratification on 14 November.

However, many of the provisions of the Charter can be carried out even without its formal effectivity. The terms of reference of the regional human rights body are already being worked out by a task force. A "scorecard" has been devised to keep track of member countries' compliance with ASEAN commitments, at least in the economic area. The United States, Japan and Australia have appointed ambassadors to ASEAN. Member states are designating permanent representatives to the Association. The search has begun for the two additional Deputy Secretary-Generals provided for in the Charter. The ASEAN Secretary-General, Dr Surin Pitsuwan, is exercising the expanded mandate that the Charter gives him. The ASEAN calendar is being adjusted according to the Charter's provisions.

Will it all work? The Charter is only a tool. All depends on how member countries use it. There are grounds for optimism. As the former Secretary-General, Ong Keng Yong, has pointed out, face is important in ASEAN, and the monitoring and reporting process provided for in the Charter involves face.

With the Charter as a tool, ASEAN needs to work even more effectively than in the past, as it faces numerous challenges in the coming year.

One of them is the current turmoil in the financial markets and economic health of the United States and Western Europe, leading markets for ASEAN's export-oriented economies. ASEAN should be thinking of what to do about the fallout in East Asia of America's and Europe's financial and economic troubles. It should also be encouraging more forcefully its members to undertake the necessary domestic reforms to weather economic instability. In light of the collapse of the Doha Round of multilateral trade negotiations, ASEAN should be working hard to ensure continued access of Southeast Asian exports to overseas markets and hasten the integra-tion of Southeast Asian, as well as the East Asian, economies. Meanwhile, the rise of energy prices demands both short-term and long-term cooperative measures. At the same time, non-traditional security threats such as terrorism, pollution, pandemics and natural disasters hang over ASEAN's head, requiring cooperative responses.

The defining strategic relationship of our time is that between China and the United States. With a new President to manage that relationship from the U.S. side, ASEAN has to make its thinking clearly felt on this vital issue. Japan too has a new leader at the helm to navigate the choppy political waters of Sino-Japanese relations, which are of critical importance to ASEAN and Southeast Asia.

Many of these imperatives require regional commitments, others political cohesion. All call for a stronger sense of regional identity among policy-makers and the citizens of ASEAN. If the ASEAN Charter can help the member countries comply with their commitments, strengthen their cohesion and deepen their sense of regional identity, we can truly say that the Charter works.

UNITED STATES-SOUTHEAST ASIA RELATIONS
By Satu P. Limaye

The new U.S. administration of Mr Barack Obama will inherit a relationship with Southeast Asia that is generally stronger — both at the bilateral level and the ASEAN/regional level — than is often portrayed both in regional capitals and in Washington D.C. U.S.-Southeast Asia relations are not irritant or problem-free. But significant change has occurred since the early dissonances over the Bush administration talking darkly of China as a "strategic competitor" and of crusades and "you are with us or against us" in the "war on terror" after the Al Qaeda attacks of 11 September 2001. Actual policy, even if occasionally clumsy diplomatically, has been sober and underlying structural opportunities are being taken advantage of.

At the same time, there will be opportunities for the new administration to make policy adjustments, symbolic changes and even some important substantive departures that will further enhance U.S. relations with Southeast Asia.

Three structural changes in U.S.-Southeast Asia relations are especially promising. First, the asymmetry in U.S. engagement with maritime and mainland Southeast Asia, a function of history including the Vietnam War and communist takeovers, is being reduced. Deputy Secretary of State John Negroponte's visit to Vietnam, Cambodia, Thailand and Laos in September 2008 is a recent high point of an incremental but steady increase in engagement on both traditional and non-traditional security cooperation with Hanoi, Phnom Penh and Vientiane. The exception is Myanmar; and that will not change until the oppressive regime changes its approach.

The reduction in the gap in U.S. engagement with mainland and maritime Southeast Asia is important because it not only improves bilateral relations with individual members of ASEAN with whom the U.S. has been estranged, but also because it indirectly contributes to ASEAN unity and efforts at integration. Simultaneously, the U.S. has continued to work effectively across a range of cooperative activities with long-standing allies and partners such as Thailand, the Philippines, Singapore, Malaysia and Brunei, while pursuing new openings with Indonesia. No matter how much effort the U.S. expends in improving bilateral ties across the region, however, outcomes will be shaped by the political and economic dynamics *within* Southeast Asian countries (e.g., Thailand, Malaysia and Indonesia after the 2009 elections) as well.

A second important gain has been U.S. efforts to cooperate with ASEAN as an organization as it moves towards implementing its goal of becoming a political, security and cultural community by 2015. The new U.S. administration will take office following ASEAN's expected ratification of its charter at its scheduled December 2008 Summit. The appointment by the U.S. of an ambassador to ASEAN, the first ASEAN dialogue partner to take this step, is an indication of American commitment to ASEAN integration. U.S. support for ASEAN integration is not contingent upon the charter's ratification, and therefore the new administration will likely remain committed to supporting ASEAN's integration through the ADVANCE programme which commits some US$7 million, particularly for activities towards an ASEAN economic community.

A third underlying positive change has been the favourable calibration of competing factors that drive U.S. policy towards Southeast Asia. The U.S. juggles bilateral, global and wider Asia-Pacific considerations as it deals with the region. During the post-war period, bilateralism at one end and globalism at the other has tended to cause swings in U.S. approaches. Today, U.S. policy towards Southeast Asia better incorporates regional considerations including the role of China, the threat of terrorism and, as noted, ASEAN's own moves towards integration and community. The net effect is to provide ballast for overall U.S.-Southeast Asia ties.

But most importantly, the new U.S. administration will have the opportunity to address several pending policy opportunities such as holding a U.S.-ASEAN summit, U.S. signature/ratification of ASEAN's Treaty of Amity and Cooperation (TAC) and a decision regarding attendance at the East Asian Summit (an option for the U.S. only if it signs the TAC).

Given U.S. domestic and foreign policy priorities, immediate and favourable decisions on these policy directions would be a surprise. However, the *zeitgeist* increasingly favours movement on all three fronts. A meeting between the new U.S. President and ASEAN leaders — even if the modalities of such a meeting have to be finessed due to the presence of Myanmar — is quite likely, perhaps on the sidelines of the Singapore APEC Summit scheduled for late 2009. After all, the Bush administration had agreed to such a summit before having to cancel it — for reasons not related to U.S.-ASEAN relations. There is also growing bipartisan support for U.S. signing the TAC. Signature of TAC looms as increasingly likely, though opponents within the bureaucracy and Congress

UNITED STATES-SOUTHEAST ASIA RELATIONS (continued)

do exist. Just how much exertion will be made on this effort depends heavily on the Congressional and overall foreign and domestic policy situation. In any case, ratification does not loom as likely — and the U.S. understands that ASEAN places a premium on the TAC signature. Views on attendance at the East Asia Summit (EAS) are mixed, with some arguing for a U.S. presence, and others opposed. Here again, depending upon conditions, an American version of the "ASEAN way" is possible under which the U.S. will be represented by an observer or senior official but not likely the U.S. President.

The new U.S. administration will also have an opportunity to avoid some of the missteps of its predecessor, such as not attending key regional meetings and postponing planned summits. But to be fair, the process of responding to Southeast Asian sensitivities has already begun. For example, Secretary of Defense Robert Gates did not use the "T-word" — terrorism — once during his prepared remarks at the annual Shangri-la Dialogue in July 2008. The administration has also been low-key about domestic political perturbations in the region. And perhaps most importantly, President Bush, in his speech in Thailand in July 2008, indicated that despite America's "complex relations with China", the U.S. seeks to have constructive relations with that country, remain fully engaged across Asia and reinforce long-standing alliances and form new democratic partnerships (presumably he meant India and Indonesia especially). If this is the agenda that even with different words shapes the next administration's policies — and it likely will — then the combination of structural changes, policy changes and tone augur well for U.S.-Southeast Asia relations.

The new U.S. administration has an opportunity to build on robust fundamentals. Some of the ways it can do so are by holding a carefully constructed U.S.-ASEAN summit, signing TAC and having representation — not necessarily the President — at the next East Asia Summit. But the most important way in which good U.S.-Southeast Asia ties will progress is if all houses are in order — providing the domestic prosperity and stability that will permit attention to and engagement in enhanced U.S.-Southeast Asia relations.

SOUTHEAST ASIA'S QUEST FOR ENERGY SECURITY: COOPERATION AND TENSIONS

By Andrew Symon

E nergy issues have never been so much at the centre of ASEAN concerns as they are today. Greater cooperation for energy security, energy ministers declared in Bangkok in August 2008, was "a pathway to building the ASEAN Economic Community".

But translating aspirations into changes in energy production and consumption patterns and relations between states is a long process. And some commentators also warn that energy anxieties can introduce tensions between countries and even pose the risk of "resources wars". Countering this is the argument that in addressing energy challenges, including the environmental sustainability of energy use, countries must forge stronger cooperation.

So what is case for Southeast Asia in 2009–2010 and beyond? Unquestionably, energy needs are fostering new links. In the Greater Mekong Subregion (GMS), cross-border transmission lines are emerging which may one day support an integrated power system. Vietnam will soon sell electricity to Cambodia through a line under construction to Phnom Penh, enabling development of a desperately needed power grid for southeast Cambodia.

Vietnam itself already purchases electricity from southern China. Links are also being put in place between Thailand and Cambodia, with supply planned from eastern Thailand to Siem Reap and the Cambodian western region, and from southwest Cambodia to Thailand from a large coal-fired plant. Power export from Laos to Thailand, which first began in 1998, is also expanding. With its extensive hydro resources, Laos would like to position itself as the "battery" of the GMS, and also wants to supply Vietnam and Cambodia. Myanmar may also supply power to Thailand from hydro-dams on the Salween River complementing its existing piped gas supply to Thailand.

But a common GMS power market is a distant vision. To move from one way cross-border supply to a single region-wide power system analogous to a national system, governments will have to pool sovereignty and institute a common liberalized and competitive power market. Nevertheless, the GMS's power links point to a level of cooperation that would have been impossible to imagine twenty years ago in the aftermath of the Indochinese conflicts.

The story though is not all roses. There are worries that China's ambitious hydropower expansion programme on the upper Mekong will damage the lower riparian ecology and harm the millions of people who derive their livelihoods from the river system. And in August 2008, record seasonal river flooding was

SOUTHEAST ASIA'S QUEST FOR ENERGY SECURITY (continued)

blamed on the dams releasing too much water into already high rivers filled by monsoon storms. While the Mekong River Commission found this not to be the case, the event still galvanized criticism of China's dams.

Intra-regional energy links may also be stymied by government efforts to ensure supply for domestic markets first of all. In Indonesia natural gas and coal producers must now reserve large shares of production for domestic supply. While these domestic market obligations (DMO) have long existed for oil, they are new for gas and coal. Rising local demand and limits to new resource discoveries, means that Jakarta no longer assumes that the archipelago can be an ever abundant source of energy exports. And this is true for Southeast Asia as a whole. The region is a net oil importer and this dependency is growing.

Some see these DMOs as economic nationalism. DMOs have introduced uncertainty among buyers of Indonesian coal and gas. In Southeast Asia, Singapore has become very dependent on Indonesian supply on top of small supply from Malaysia, taking pipeline gas from south Sumatra and offshore west Natuna in the South China Sea. Eighty per cent of Singapore's power generation is gas fuelled. While supply is contracted until around 2020, it may be that by the time Singapore wants to renew contracts, Jakarta may feel the gas must be dedicated to the domestic market. Given this possibility, Singapore is putting in place another supply option: from 2012, it will also import gas in shipped liquefied form (LNG) under a contract with British Gas signed in April 2008.

Nowhere is nationalism more evident than in maritime boundary disputes. The contested claims in the South China Sea around the Spratly Islands have come into sharp relief again due to rising energy prices. Beijing is stridently declaring that exploration off the southeast coast of Vietnam by several companies, including BP, ONGC of India, and ExxonMobil of the U.S., is in Chinese waters. Hope that the three-year-old joint seismic programme by the state oil companies of China, Vietnam and the Philippines in the eastern Spratly's region would provide a model for cooperative development has also been dashed: the agreement, which expired at the end of June 2008, is not being extended.

There are also ongoing petroleum based disputes between Brunei and Malaysia over the maritime border between the east Malaysian state of Sabah and Brunei, and between Malaysia and Indonesia over an offshore area between the southeast corner of Sabah and northeast Kalimantan.

New attention is also being placed on the large, prospective Overlapping Claims Area (OCA) between Thailand and Cambodia in the Gulf of Thailand following the tensions in 2008 between Phnom Penh and Bangkok over land border issues centred on the Preah Vihear temple. Given the sabre rattling that took place over Preah Vihear, especially by the Thais, it is hard to see early resolution of the OCA, even though much more is at stake economically.

Yet, energy demand should eventually pressure governments to compromise. In the case of the OCA, gas and oil unlocked would be of huge benefit for the Thai market. Thailand faces an ever widening gap between existing supplies of gas and power demand growth, while oil imports for transport continue to grow ever larger. And for very poor Cambodia, petroleum revenues should be an enormous boost. Much will depend on the Thai political situation returning to some normality.

That joint agreements can be reached is shown by the Malaysia-Thai Joint Development Area and the Malaysia-Vietnamese Commercial Agreement Area in the Gulf of Thailand. Negotiated in the mid to late 1990s, both are now producing oil and also piping gas to Malaysia, Thailand, and also Vietnam.

As the quest of energy security mounts, Southeast Asia will face a mixture of tensions and imperatives for cooperation. The latest development to bring these dynamics into play is the thrust for the region's first nuclear power plants by 2020, led by Vietnam and Indonesia. Thailand, Malaysia and the Philippines are also looking at nuclear power.

While nuclear power may be part of the answer to demand in a world of higher fossil fuel prices — and in a way that reduces growth of climate change inducing carbon dioxide emissions — there are serious safety, environmental and non-proliferation issues. Singapore is one that has made plain its concern.

In Indonesia, nuclear power could be a major issue in the national and presidential elections in 2009 as there is growing public opposition to the technocrats' plans for a first plant to be built on the north coast of central Java by 2017. And regionally, over the next year or so, the question of how nuclear power can be best managed is sure to rise higher in intergovernmental forums, adding to a range of energy and related issues facing ASEAN.

THE ASEAN-10

Pushpa Thambipillai • Sophal Ear •
Bernhard Platzdasch • Martin Stuart-Fox •
Johan Saravanamuttu • Robert H. Taylor •
Felipe B. Miranda • Terence Chong •
Supinya Klangnarong • David Koh

Brunei Darussalam

Brunei Darussalam's name — the Abode of Peace — is an apt one, for compared to some other Southeast Asian countries, it represents a model of stability.

The monarchical system is well entrenched, and will continue for the foreseeable future. Neither the current ruler, Sultan Haji Hassanal Bolkiah, the 29th Sultan in the lineage, nor the Crown Prince and Deputy Sultan, Haji Al-Muhtadee Billah, is in any hurry to change the national political order. The 62-year-old Sultan is relatively young in comparison with other monarchs around the world, and will likely to continue in his position; this is also the desire of his subjects who consider him the peoples' monarch. The father-son team will continue as Prime Minister and Senior Minister, and another member of the royal family, Prince Mohamed Bolkiah, is also likely to continue as Foreign Minister.

That there will be some generational change in the political system sometime in the next decade is evinced by the fact that the Crown Prince has assumed a more active and prominent role. For instance, Prince Al-Muhtadee Billah addressed the new session of the United Nations General Assembly (UNGA) in September 2008, a task usually undertaken by the Sultan himself or the Foreign Minister. The visit

BRUNEI DARUSSALAM

Land Area:	5,770 sq. km.
Population:	381,371
Capital:	Bandar Seri Begawan
Type of Government:	Monarchy
Head of State and Government:	Sultan Haji Hassanal Bolkiah Muizzaddin Waddaulah
Currency Used:	Brunei dollar
US$ exchange rate on 18 November 2008:	US$1 = B$1.50

also exposed him to other high-level diplomatic activity including the ASEAN foreign ministers meeting, the special Commonwealth Heads of Government Meeting and dinners hosted by President George W. Bush and the Speaker of the UNGA. Those occasions did not fail to impress television viewers back home, who could see their young prince taking on important tasks of statecraft to equip himself for weighty responsibilities in the future.

The current monarch will continue to exercise a direct influence on the various facets of the state's development as he is both head of state and of government. His schedules include receiving visiting leaders and other dignitaries. He personally conducts international diplomacy on overseas trips, while allocating some of the diplomatic tasks to the Crown Prince. He exercises firm control over the political and administrative matters of the state. The August 2008 cabinet reshuffle, in which three ministers were reassigned, is an indication that he closely follows ministerial performances.

The Sultan continues to undertake a direct interest in social and economic matters of the state. In 2008 the two main theses of his addresses have been the eradication of poverty and the importance of food security. In a country that boasts a per capita income of around

US$20,000, it is disheartening for Bruneians to find several hundred "hard core" poor who live in dilapidated dwellings and survive on meager incomes. Thus national policies in 2009–2010 will address the related issues of eradicating poverty, extending agricultural productivity, providing adequate housing and increasing employment opportunities.

The state's appointed legislative assembly meets early in the year to deliberate and approve the annual national budget. The 2008 session was no different and it appears it will maintain its present format over the next couple of years. The selected backbenchers will continue to be the only source of public query or criticism of government ministers and their policies.

The generation that was in public service during the post independence years has recently retired and a new generation of younger and better educated personnel is taking charge. The net result will be a more efficient administrative system in the next three to five years. Regular reviews and training is being pursued in meeting that target. Another area that will see better management is the e-government sector that has been introduced in the last several years in selected administrative areas. It has faced immense problems in its start-up stages and will need a few more years before it will function efficiently. An improved system will also facilitate an efficient consumer billing system for water and electricity, which has cost the public authorities B$226 million in unpaid bills. The large deficit in revenue, a reflection of weak administrative and social practices, is cause for concern.

The government is concerned with conserving the country's natural resources, primarily oil and gas, on which Brunei is dependent on for its development projects. Prudent public policy expenditure will ensure that Brunei is able to conserve its resources without over exploitation, while continuing to provide the free or subsidized social services that citizens have grown to expect from the state.

Although there are no imminent threats to national security, adequate support will be maintained for the armed forces, police and other enforcement agencies like customs, immigration and anti-drug agencies. The armed forces will experience modest expansion in terms of personnel while concentrating on increasing professionalization. This will be achieved partly through cooperation and training with neighbouring countries as well as traditional partners like Australia, Great Britain and the United States. The major defence focus for Brunei is its vital maritime economic zones, home to lucrative offshore energy resources. Non-traditional security issues — including illegal immigration, smuggling and narcotics trafficking — are other issues the armed forces are tasked with addressing. As Bruneians enjoy a higher per capita income than their immediate neighbours, and have access to subsidized commodities like rice, sugar and petrol, there will be continual attempts to smuggle those items out.

Internal security issues such as political opposition, civil unrest or religious and ethnic disturbances are absent in Brunei. Religious propagation and practice, and the strong adherence in the approved Suni tradition, provides the overarching influence for a society built on the Malay Islamic Monarchy ideology. For any disturbance to the status-quo there is always the Internal Security Act that can be used to punish or "rehabilitate" wrongdoers.

As a small political unit sandwiched amongst larger neighbours, it is necessary for Brunei to integrate itself with the political and security policies of ASEAN, while maintaining its cherished bilateral and multilateral linkages outside the Association, including, for example, its long time ally Britain. ASEAN will be its major source of collective engagement as evidenced by the fact that Brunei was one of the first countries to ratify the ASEAN Charter barely three months after its signing at the 2007 Summit. Brunei will maintain its usual warm relations with its external partners, notably Malaysia and Singapore, and will settle its territorial disputes through diplomacy, even if this entails protracted negotiations.

Cambodia

Coming on the heels of an overwhelming National Assembly (NA) victory (90 out of 123 seats — an increase of 17 seats over 2003) in

CAMBODIA

Land Area:	181,040 sq. km.
Population:	14 million
Capital:	Phnom Penh
Type of Government:	Parliamentary democracy with constitutional monarch
Head of State:	King Norodom Sihamoni
Prime Minister:	Hun Sen
Next Election:	January 2011 (Senate)
Currency Used:	Riel
US$ exchange rate on 18 November 2008:	US$1 = 4,188 riel

the 27 July 2008 elections, the ruling Cambodian People's Party (CPP) will govern Cambodia in the next five years with little-to-no-effective political opposition. The political landscape in 2009–2010 is likely to be an extension of business as usual: the CPP will control a political system absent checks and balances with an increasingly marginalized free press; Prime Minister Hun Sen will continue to consolidate power politically and with the help of his 4,000 strong personal bodyguard unit, Brigade 70; and the opposition Sam Rainsy Party (SRP) will be further marginalized having increased its electoral margin by only two NA seats to twenty-six. Progress on the new government's five-year plan — announced at the first cabinet meeting held on 26 September 2008 — which includes the promotion of the rule of law, protection of human rights and democracy, and an increase in the effectiveness of public services, is unlikely to be impressive given the government's long-standing record of poor governance and lack of political will.

While double-digit economic growth in recent years may suggest the rise of a developmental state, the government has little incentive to move forward on combating corruption and addressing civil service reform given continued inflows of foreign aid and Foreign Direct Investment (FDI), especially from South Korea and China. In particular, the ruling CPP's commitment and capacity to address the effectiveness of public services — indeed national development itself — in the next two years are predicated on improvement in domestic revenues, especially tax revenues, which have stagnated despite tremendous economic growth since 2002.

The average civil servant's salary remains extremely low — less than garment workers who currently make a minimum of circa US$50 per month — and is insufficient to cover basic living expenses, forcing civil servants to moonlight or resort to corruption. But progress on the National Programme for Administrative Reform, approved by the government in 1999, has been rudderless given an entrenched patronage system that has permeated every aspect of the bureaucracy since its inception. Indeed, there is a general lack of incentive by the CPP to effect reforms as this would require it to dismantle the lucrative patronage system that has flourished in the last decade and a half.

The long-awaited anti-graft legislation has been in draft form for more than a decade and there is little indication that a meaningful and enforceable bill will be passed in 2009. Consequently, corruption, the canary in the mineshaft of effective governance in Cambodia, may in fact worsen in the short-to-medium term as FDI grows. In 2008, the country ranked 166th out of 180 on Transparency International's Corruption Perception Index, placing it in the bottom 10th percentile, but in 2005, the first year in which it was ranked, Cambodia was near the 18th percentile. Thus, perceptions of Cambodian corruption have worsened over the past three years.

Human rights concerns will continue to be a source of social instability in 2009–2010 and a focal point of contention with the international community. The issue of land grabbing, whereby tycoons and government officials illegally expropriate public and private land, has long simmered. Due to the unprecedented increase in the value of real estate in Phnom Penh, Siem Reap (the gateway to Angkor Wat), and the coastal city of Sihanoukville, this trend will only increase in the foreseeable future. Hundreds if not thousands of peasants, some travelling hundreds of kilometres by foot, have converged on Phnom Penh and the Prime Minister's residence seeking redress. While Hun Sen has repeatedly and very publicly demanded that land grabbing cease, these activities have continued unabated. The capacity of the government to address the issue is questionable given a thoroughly captured judicial system and an environment of impunity for well-connected elites. It is highly likely that land grabs will continue.

The government's commitment to improving human rights is questionable and will further generate contention with the international community. The September 2008 resignation of Yash Ghai, the UN's special envoy for human rights to Cambodia, after three years of strained relations with Hun Sen, underscores the confrontational approach the government has taken towards the international body and NGOs over this issue. This relationship will most likely worsen in the next two years due to the government's perennial desire to shutdown the Office of the High Commissioner for Human Rights (OHCHR). While it has agreed to retain the OHCHR for an additional year, the government may yet succeed in achieving its goal.

As has been the case since Cambodia's transition to a parliamentary democracy in 1993, the role of the opposition will remain nominal. With the implosion of the royalist Funcinpec Party which lost twenty-four of its twenty-six NA seats, the SRP, led by the outspoken former Funcinpec Finance Minister Sam Rainsy, remains the primary bulwark against the CPP. But the SRP and other smaller opposition parties such as the Human Rights Party, which has three NA seats, have very little leverage in a political system dominated by Hun Sen's CPP. A concentration in urban areas and a reliance on charismatic leaders rather than a coherent strategy impedes the opposition's ability to garner widespread support. Tremendous gains by the CPP in Phnom Penh suggest the erosion of urban support for the SRP in the July 2008 elections.

Several pressure points will prove a challenge for the ruling party in 2009. First, while border tensions with Thailand have provided a boost to the popularity of the CPP by inflaming nationalism, deteriorating relations with its neighbours does not serve the country's interests in the long term. Nationalism on both sides of the border over the disputed ownership of Preah Vihear temple and surrounding lands has the potential of escalating into armed conflict. The selection of Somchai Wongsawat as Thailand's new Prime Minister and the potential for political stability in 2009 in Bangkok may serve to calm tensions.

Second, unchecked inflation, officially 20.94 per cent between January and July 2008, in addition to a slowdown in the global economy, may trigger social instability. The price of rice has nearly doubled in the past year, and anecdotal reports suggest that villagers have had to ration their food supply and consume lower-grade food items. Moreover, with a predominantly young and restless workforce, a cooling economy and an inevitable slowdown garments and tourism — Cambodia's top two sectors — may result in social unrest. It remains to be seen how the ruling CPP can adapt to these challenges in the coming years.

Despite these challenges, one thing will remain constant: Hun Sen's grip on power. Indeed, the strongman, who became the word's youngest prime minister in 1985 at the age of 33, stated last year: "If I am still alive, I will continue to stand as a candidate until I am 90." Short of a fundamental change in the political system such as regime change, unchecked social instability, or ill health, there is little doubt as to who will run Cambodia through 2010 and far beyond. As such, the prospects for political stability in Cambodia in the next two years are excellent.

Indonesia

In 2009 Indonesian politics will be dominated by parliamentary and presidential elections that will result in another coalition government though with a slightly different vote allocation among the leading parties.

Two likely differences can be anticipated. First, the PDIP (Indonesian Democratic Party of Struggle), led by Megawati Soekarnoputri, may well replace Golkar, led by Jusuf Kalla, as the largest party in parliament (DPR). An indication for this was given by Golkar's defeat in a number of polls in 2008 in regions that were formerly party strongholds. A second

INDONESIA

Land Area:	1,919,440 sq. km.
Population:	237.512 million
Capital:	Jakarta
Type of Government:	Presidential Republic
Head of State:	Dr Susilo Bambang Yudhoyono
Next Election:	April 2009 (Parliamentary), July 2009 (Presidential)
Currency Used:	Rupiah
US$ exchange rate on 18 November 2008:	US$1 = 11,655 rupiah

vital shift concerns the Islamist parties. PPP (Unity and Development Party), the only Islamist party of the New Order era and for some time the country's largest Islamist party, is bound to lose its leading position to PKS (Justice Welfare Party). PKS's replacement of the PPP as Indonesia's largest Islamist party reflects a growing conservatism in Indonesian Islam, a trend that has affected most Muslim organizations in the country.

There are several possible scenarios for a future government. Golkar has been the backbone of Yudhoyono's coalition government since Kalla became party chairman in late 2004. This support, however, was eroded in 2008 and is likely to be further put to the test in the run-up to the polls. Golkar today is not the unified and centralized organization it was under President Soeharto. Some sections of the party want Kalla to step forward as Golkar's own presidential contender. Others have been challenging his party leadership because of their own political ambitions. Significantly, in mid-2008, Yudhoyono raised fuel prices by nearly thirty per cent in order to prevent a budgetary crisis, leading many Golkar figures to fear that this unpopular decision could hurt the party at the polls.

Nevertheless, the likely scenario — especially if PDIP outperforms Golkar — is that Yudhoyono and Golkar will renew their partnership. Many of its leaders are adamant about repositioning Golkar as a governing party. A PDIP-Golkar partnership is unlikely as Megawati has made plain that she is only interested in the top post. She might, however, still be able to pull off an electoral victory by benefiting from a public perception that Yudhoyono has not delivered on his pledge to improve the lives of ordinary Indonesians.

Approaching the elections, Yudhoyono will attempt to avoid any further steps that put him in danger of losing votes. At the same time, leaders from all parties will be increasingly alert not to be associated with unpopular government policies. As such, Megawati has already announced that she will not raise fuel prices if elected. As in 1999 and 2004, campaign issues will centre on those likely to garner votes. These are mainly connected with the price of basic commodities such as food and fuel and the creation of jobs. All this is indicative of a rising pragmatism among Indonesian politicians.

Overall, almost eleven years into *reformasi*, Indonesia is an established, vibrant democracy. This distinguishes the country from other democracies in the region; democracies that looked more promising a few years back such as Thailand and Malaysia. One central feature is the durability of Indonesian parties. All of the main parties that contested the first *reformasi* elections in 1999 have survived. Moreover, Indonesia remains one of the few Muslim-majority countries with a stable democracy. All parties channel their goals strictly through democratic institutions, including the Islamist parties. There are no parties with a radical agenda. A slip back to authoritarian and military rule appears out of the question for the time being. A large scale terrorist attack is seemingly unlikely. Indonesia might also be able to advance its ambitions to play a bigger role on the world stage, though realistically speaking its ability to influence global issues, such as Palestine, the Korean Peninsula and Iran's nuclear programme, remains limited.

While Indonesian democracy is stable, many weaknesses and shortcomings are likely to persist for the foreseeable future. As such they will continue to impact negatively on the performance of future governments.

The first shortcoming is that *reformasi* governments will continue to consist of multi-party coalitions with no single party enjoying an absolute majority. This renders coalitions brittle, and negotiations over legislation tend to be convoluted and lengthy. Second, while the main parties have proved to be durable, they also remain prone to factionalism. Worst affected by this has been the PKB (National Awakening Party). The bitter power struggles in the party have cost it much support and it is expected to suffer a drop in votes in the 2009 elections.

Third, most Indonesian parties suffer from weak leadership. At the same time, surveys have indicated that many Indonesians continue to be transfixed with individual leaders. A handful of the old *reformasi* elite are still capable of drawing sizeable followings. The foremost example is PDIP's Megawati who looks like the only serious contender for the presidency despite a lackluster performance as head of state in 2001–2004. The list of legislative candidates for the 2009 elections, however, indicates a gradual change of guard. Local elections in 2008 signalled to party elites that there is a strong desire for new and younger leaders. Most parties, including Golkar and PDIP, have responded by appointing a large number of new legislative candidates, many of whom are from a non-political background. Usually, these new entries are selected on the basis of their popularity. Hence, whereas new leaders will emerge over the next few years, it is not guaranteed that they will be able to execute better leadership.

Fourth, Indonesia's party financing system is ineffective and one of the areas in urgent need of reform. 2009 will see a continuation of the anti-corruption drive that has been characteristic of the *reformasi* years. Indonesian legislators tend to be held in low public esteem, and media and criticism sometimes borders on the excessive. This criticism tends to neglect the deeper causes of corruption as party officials are often forced to look for alternative ways to raise money. So although party financing is a major problem, there are few signs that it will be tackled decisively in 2009–2010.

Fifth, the sweeping decentralization initiatives have resulted in corrupt local governments. The performance of local governments often remains poor and the precise distribution of power between central and local governments unclear. These challenges, too, are unlikely to be overcome any time soon.

Lastly, and more broadly, there seems to be some ideological confusion at the state level. This is grounded in the growing need for the government to cater to Islamic sentiments, an enduring commitment to pluralist Pancasila ideals and increasingly strained inter-faith relations. Signs of this are the government's ambivalent ruling on the Islamic Ahmadiyah sect, the recently passed "anti-pornography bill" and an initiative by the Head of the Constitutional Court, Dr Mahfud MD, to re-examine various shari'ah by-laws that had been implemented during recent years. All these are far-reaching issues which are pending clarification. How the next government deals with these questions will give a clearer picture of the country's stance towards religious tolerance and pluralism.

Laos

Politics in the Lao People's Democratic Republic (LPDR) is almost entirely opaque to outside observers. Nothing is reported in the tightly controlled Lao media by way of political commentary, let alone speculation. Diplomats pick up rumours and talk to each other, but no one knows what is happening behind the scenes.

Part of the reason for this lack of political transparency is the legacy of history: the ruling Lao People's Revolutionary Party (LPRP) was always highly secretive — indeed it hid its very existence during its thirty-year struggle (1945–1975) to seize power — and it has remained so ever since. But another reason has to do with Lao political culture, and how power is concentrated and used.

As in other Southeast Asian countries, especially the Theravada Buddhist mainland states, power is concentrated by building patronage networks of allies and clients who are prepared to provide political support when it counts. Clients must derive appropriate benefits, but

LAOS

Land Area:	236,800 sq. km.
Population:	6.52 million
Capital:	Vientiane
Type of Government:	Communist People's Democratic Republic
Head of State:	Lt. Gen. Choummaly Sayasone
Prime Minister:	Bouason Bouphavan
Next Election:	2011
Currency Used:	Kip
US$ exchange rate on 18 November 2008:	US$1 = 8,754 kip

relationships are personal: they take time to establish, through face-to-face contact. The patronage networks of senior figures in the Political Bureau have been built up over years.

When Lt. Gen. Choummaly Sayasone took over the presidency of both the LPDR and the LPRP from General Khamtay Siphandone in 2006, his ascendency continued the dominance of both the military and the old revolutionary generation. This is evident from the line-up of the Politburo: the next four positions are also held by former military officers in their seventies. The Prime Minister, Bouasone Bouphavan, aged fifty-four, comes in only at number seven.

The hope that with Bouasone's appointment power would pass to the next generation of younger and better educated Party leaders was never, therefore, likely — at least not in the short term. Bouasone, despite years of service as a Party official, had no well defined constituency of his own, for Party members were divided between rival patronage networks. This is why nothing has come of his pledge to the National Assembly that he would introduce more transparency into government and curb corruption: he has yet to build his own patronage network.

This has taken time. The old generals have a hold on power that is not easily undermined. Bouasone has sought support from the next generation of younger and better educated Party members who make up not just much of the current ministry, but also deputy ministers and departmental heads with administrative and technical experience. He has also wooed younger intellectuals who have returned to Laos with degrees from overseas universities to teach at the National University of Laos.

Bouasone has also sought the support of his former rival Foreign Minister Dr Thongloun Sisoulith, and of Thongban Sengaphone the increasingly powerful Minister for Security (formerly the Interior Ministry), who is in charge of the police and secret service, and so could provide a useful counterbalance to the continued dominance of the military.

It is unclear as yet whether this strategy is on track, or whether his own support network will be sufficiently cohesive to provide Bouasone with the political base he needs. At present he is not in a position to challenge President Choummaly. And other powerful Politburo members may want to stand in his way, including former Interior Minister Lt. Gen. Asang Laoly and former Foreign Minister Somsavat Lengsavad. Asang can call on old loyalties in the security services, which could restrain Thongban from forming an alliance with Bouasone, while Somsavat has the backing of important foreign business interests, particularly Chinese, whose investments in Laos he has facilitated.

Foreign influence also plays a significant, if equally opaque, role in internal Lao politics. The principal players are Vietnam and China. Lao Party cadres still attend ideological training courses in Vietnam, which means that the Vietnamese are well informed about the upper echelons of the LPRP, and have a much better understanding of how Lao politics works than any other country.

Vietnam has two principal political interests in Laos. Of primary importance is the maintenance of Vietnamese influence, which depends on having close party-to-party ties. An equal interest, therefore, is the survival of the LPRP as the sole political party in Laos. Accordingly,

Vietnamese advice has as one of its goals the strengthening of the LPRP. And that requires limiting both personal factionalism and high-level corruption. Reportedly Bouasone enjoys Vietnamese support because Hanoi believes he is best able to carry through Party reforms required to curb the growing corruption, and the popular cynicism with regard to the Party that results.

China also provides ideological and managerial training for Lao cadres, along with substantial aid and investment. The Chinese helped Laos during the Asian economic crisis of the late 1990s, and more recently the China Development Bank brokered a deal whereby a consortium of three Chinese companies will build a new sports stadium in time for when Laos hosts the 2009 Southeast Asian games — in return for a long-term lease of land in Vientiane on which to develop a large housing estate.

Opportunities for Chinese commercial penetrations of Laos have been provided by improved river and road access from southern China into northern Laos, and a large market in Vientiane in which predominantly Chinese merchants sell Chinese products. Chinese companies have been granted mining concessions and land for agricultural and forestry plantations. China has also granted loans under favourable terms and cancelled debt.

As Prime Minister, Bouasone has to sign off on major projects and inter-state agreements. His willingness to do so has gained him Chinese support. The support of both Hanoi and Beijing has strengthened Bouasone's position in the LPRP, but not yet to the extent of being able to drive his own programme.

A continuing problem for the government is the relationship between the centre and the provinces, which have always enjoyed a degree of autonomy in running their affairs. A recent matter of contention has been over the granting of land concessions at rates the central government believes have been too low (in return for bribes to provincial authorities). The government also wants to extract higher royalties and taxes from foreign mining companies, a move likely to have the reverse effect by discouraging large-scale and long-term investment. Both these matters have yet to be resolved, and will be watched with interest over the coming year, as an indicator of where the government is heading.

The government certainly needs to raise more revenue in order to fund its social programmes. Spending on education and health have been abysmally low, but are slated to increase in 2009 when the Nam Theun hydroelectric project comes on-stream. Under terms negotiated with the World Bank, a substantial portion of revenue from sales of electricity to Thailand will be directed to poverty alleviation. Implementation, however — as always in Laos — will be another matter.

In the meantime, politics are likely to continue as usual: that is, as a competition between powerful patronage networks for access to economic resources. It is just this competition that stimulates the corruption that is corroding the Party. Powerful figures look after themselves and their clients, with little thought for the national interest. Take the agreement said to have been concluded for a Chinese and Thai consortium to develop a large bauxite deposit in southern Laos. A Lao company will have a ten per cent stake, owned not by the Lao government, but by interests linked to the patronage network of former President Khamtay Siphandone. Meanwhile Khamtay's son, the governor of Champassak province, is tipped to be appointed as a minister in the prime minister's office, where he will be in an excellent position to protect his family interests.

Under these circumstances, Prime Minister Bouasone is unlikely to be able to institute any significant reforms, even if he wants to, and even with Vietnamese and Chinese support.

Malaysia

After the political tsunami triggered by the 8 March 2008 general election, the face of Malaysian politics may have undergone more than a cosmetic adjustment. The newly formed People's Pact (Pakatan Rakyat, PR), comprising the National People's Justice Party (PKR), the Democratic Action Party (DAP) and the Pan-Malaysian Islamic Party (PAS), deprived the ruling National Front (Barisan Nasional, BN) of its

MALAYSIA

Land Area:	330,434 sq. km.
Population:	27.73 million
Capital:	Kuala Lumpur (Administrative capital: Putrajaya)
Type of Government:	Federated parliamentary democracy with constitutional monarchy
Head of State:	Yang Di-Pertuan Agong Tuanku Mizan Zainal Abidin
Prime Minister:	Datuk Seri Abdullah Anmad Badawi
Next Election:	2013
Currency Used:	Ringgit (RM)
US$ exchange rate on 18 November 2008:	US$1 = RM3.61

all-important two-thirds parliamentary majority and also gained control of five states. To make matters worse for the BN, former Deputy Prime Minister Anwar Ibrahim, the *de facto* leader of PR, demonstrated on 26 August that 8 March was no fluke: Anwar swept the Permatang Pauh by-election with a majority of well over 15,000 votes and was officially anointed as leader of the opposition in Parliament.

With this resounding victory in his former constituency, vacated by wife and PKR leader Wan Azizah, Anwar's moment to topple the government seemed palpable as he cleverly kept alive a strategy of baiting crossovers of BN parties and politicians from Sarawak and Sabah. However, the deadline of 16 September 2008 passed with a Parliament out of session and Anwar not making good his claim of toppling the BN. By October 2008, Anwar had put his takeover plan on the backburner. In the event, the United Malays National Organization (UMNO), re-grouped and dumped its embattled leader Abdullah Ahmad Badawi, who has turned out to be the biggest casualty of the political tsunami — Abdullah will step down in March 2009 in favour of his deputy, Najib Razak. Another casualty in the future may be the political fortunes of Abdullah's son-in-law, Khary Jamaluddin. With such major changes to the political landscape, what political repercussions and developments can one expect for Malaysian politics in 2009–2010?

First, it must be stressed that Malaysia now has a *de jure*, if still nascent, two-party (or two-coalition) system at the state level, where PR governments run five governments, namely, Selangor, Penang, Perak, Kedah and Kelantan. In these states, the BN now finds itself in the unfamiliar role of opposition, except in Kelantan where this has been the case for about two decades. One may well say that Malaysian democracy is alive and well and citizens can now have four to five years to judge four new state governments and whether to re-elect them the next time around. As such, the formalization of the People's Front as an alternative coalition to the National Front is *fait accompli*. Unlike its predecessor, the Alternative Front (Barisan Alternative) of 1998–1999, PR's governmental presence seems guaranteed for some time to come by virtue of state power. By most accounts, citizens appear to be satisfied with the performance of the PR so far.

Second, the obverse may be true for the BN coalition. It is clearly in a state of transformation if not turmoil. Already one component party, the Sabah Progressive Party (SAPP) has abandoned the pact (on 17 September 2008) while the Gerakan and even the Malaysian Chinese Association (MCA) has sounded out their deep disaffection with UMNO politics. These component parties are themselves in a state of political reinvention. One senior female leader and her supporters left the MCA and joined Anwar's party in July 2008. The suggestion by the Gerakan leader Koh Tsu Koon to have direct membership in the BN and to turn it eventually into a multiracial party hints at the current poor formula of racial power sharing within the National Front today. The leader of Sabah's native-based United Pasokmomogun Kadazandusun Murut Organization (UPKO), Bernard Dompok, has also expressed grave concern about the failure of the National Front government to deal with three urgent matters, namely, the unequal exchange of economic benefits to Sabah and its concomitant status as Malaysia's poorest state, the issue of religious freedom and the unresolved problem of the influx of more than one million illegal immigrants into Sabah.

At the federal level, the formation of a strong parliamentary opposition with 82 seats is also bound to have considerable and continued impact on the BN even without a no-confidence vote against the government. The threat of crossovers remains possible. The Malaysian budget for 2009 may be in tatters given the global financial crisis in October 2008. Ministers who are tasked to table bills will get a thorough grilling from the opposition benches. All eyes will focus on UMNO's attempt to re-establish itself with its new leader, Najib Razak, who now holds the crucial finance ministry. As Prime Minister, will Najib be able to deliver much needed reforms to the police, judiciary and civil service where Abdullah failed conspicuously? How will Najib's cabinet look after a likely reshuffle following the likely turbulent UMNO party conference in March 2009?

Whatever happens at the party conference, UMNO's position of primacy within the ruling coalition is unlikely to change. The new leadership is likely to see the continued influence (if not interference) of former Prime Minister Dr Mahathir Mohamad. Moreover, if his son, Mukhriz, assumes the leadership of the UMNO Youth Movement, he would act as a natural conduit for his father's continued influence in UMNO. Najib, as UMNO's new leader with his likely deputy Muhyiddin Yassin are bound to be more accommodating to Mahathir and his ideas as compared to Abdullah Badawi.

Not much will change with respect to parties within the PR as Anwar consolidates his leadership within the PKR while PAS and DAP, which have already held their party congresses, continue to manage government and politics within the five PR states. The much touted idea of an actual PR takeover of government remains highly unlikely in 2009 given Abdullah's departure from the scene.

Nevertheless, two major unresolved issues will continue to exercise Malaysian political actors whether in government, opposition or civil society. First, the Internal Security Act (ISA) detention of five Hindu

Rights Action Force (HINDRAF) leaders remains a problem for the government with regular vigils held to protest the use of the ISA despite the unexpected release of blogger Raja Petra after a court ruling on 7 November. Civil society groups and the opposition will continue to press for the release of the HINDRAF five while the credibility and legitimacy of the Malaysian Indian Congress (MIC) and its leader, Samy Vellu will remain in limbo until the HINDRAF issue is resolved. Malaysia has the dubious distinction of two "missing in action" abroad, *personae non grata* Mr Waytha Moorthy of HINDRAF and Mr P. Balasubramaniam, the private detective who made a statutory declaration about Najib Razak and his association with the murdered Mongolian model, Altantuya Shaariibuu.

The second most serious issue for the post-Abdullah UMNO leadership could be the dénouement of the Altantuya murder trial. Despite the unexpected acquittal on 31 October of political analyst Razak Baginda for abetment, a long trial may ensue for the two police officers whose defence has been called. This could still have grave implications for the new prime minister Najib Razak as the two officers were formerly assigned to him. Already still unverified text messages have shown Najib purportedly having correspondences with a senior lawyer over the case. Similarly, the course and outcome of Anwar's Ibrahim's sodomy trial will not only affect his own political fortunes but also his leadership of the PR. Both the leaders of the government and the opposition will have uncertain trajectories in 2009. Who will navigate through the political minefields and emerge as the victor? As Malaysians edge gingerly into 2009, a still fluid and uncertain political scenario awaits them.

Myanmar

The military government of Myanmar, the State Peace and Development Council (SPDC), looked to be unassailable at the end of 2008. Having coped with the aftermath of Cyclone Nargis — that killed more than 135,000 people and caused widespread destruction in five townships in the lower Ayeyawady delta and large parts of Yangon Division — and subsequently seen the final approval in May 2008 of a draft

MYANMAR

Land Area:	678,675 sq. km.
Population:	55.4 million (end 2006)
Capital:	Naypyitaw
Type of Government:	Military regime
Head of State:	Senior General Than Shwe
Prime Minister:	General Thein Sein
Next Election:	2010
Currency Used:	Kyat
US$ exchange rate: on 18 November 2008	US$1 = 6.57 kyat (official rate)

constitution, which firmly ensconces the military in a supererogatory position in a future political order, the oft reviled regime in Naypyitaw was impervious to attacks from its foreign and domestic political opponents. As the SPDC continued to follow its slow and deliberate road map to a "disciplined democracy" culminating in elections in 2010, exiled political activists, highly constrained domestic politicians, impotent insurgents and some Western governments were left with few options other than stunts and public relations gimmicks.

The constitution, approved by over ninety per cent of the eligible population in a referendum that was denounced as a sham by the regime's critics, holds out the prospect of limited power sharing between the army and as yet unformed political parties and former insurgent groups. The next eighteen months are likely to witness the formation of a number of parties sponsored by clients and partners of the regime. Though the regime-sponsored Union Solidarity and Development Association (USDA) is formally constrained from being converted into a political party because of a ban on civil servants becoming involved in politics, businesspersons who fund many of its activities are likely to establish parties once the regime issues a new election law. This will possibly be decreed in late 2008, to coincide with a planned visit by the United Nations Secretary-General Ban Ki-moon. Ceasefire groups that had their formal constitutional roles confirmed under the new constitution will probably also organize under the election law to ensure that they gain influence in the relevant state and regional legislatures that will be formed under the new constitution as well as in the central legislature.

In administrative terms, and in terms of the everyday life of the population, the inauguration of a new constitutional order will result in little, if any, change. Rather, the constitution will confirm the agreements and power distribution that has emerged from the reorganization of the state and army following the 1988 uprising and the abortive 1990 elections. The National League for Democracy (NLD), the party of long time detainee Daw Aung San Suu Kyi, if it decides to stand in the elections, is unlikely to be able to organize as freely and effectively as it did in 1990. However, given the party's rejection of the constitutional process that the military put in place following the failure of the NLD to accept its terms for negotiating a political transition in 1990, 2009 may well see its formal dissolution.

The SPDC's business allies demonstrated their utility to the regime in the aftermath of Cyclone Nargis. Given responsibility, along with a number of non-governmental organizations, the Buddhist monkhood, and the army itself, for the reconstruction of the most badly damaged areas under the supervision of ministers assigned to each affected township, a close working relationship between the government and the larger society was demonstrated to be effective. While not transforming the political order from the state-dominant system that Myanmar has experienced since independence, it does suggest that the beginnings of a greater degree of participation *vis-à-vis* the government is emerging within the larger civil society. Whether this trend will be allowed to continue, of course, remains unknown. Setbacks have occurred in the past as a consequence of potential assaults on the government that increase its rulers' primary concerns about regime and state security. As Senior General Than Shwe and his deputy, General Maung Aye, withdraw from power, the next generation of army officers who are now managing affairs will probably follow in the footsteps of their predecessors, being constantly alert to potential or real threats to their definition of order and stability.

The regime and its domestic and international partners will continue to wrestle with a number of ongoing and seemingly intractable issues. If resources are not generated to provide alternative livelihoods to poor people the possibility of a return to widespread opium cultivation in the Shan States remains recurrent. Problems surrounding the still unresolved issue of the so-called Rohingya-Muslim population of northern Rakhine State remain an outstanding issue, as does the continuing low-level insurgency conducted along the Thai-Myanmar border by remnants of the once powerful, but now nearly extinct, Karen National Union (KNU) army. While the more than twenty insurgent groups that have maintained ceasefire agreements with the regime since the 1990s may not have resolved all of their issues, the conclusion of the constitutional process seemingly assures that a return to open warfare on a broad scale, as happened so often in Myanmar's past, is unlikely to occur. Demobilizing the largest of the ceasefire armies, especially the Wa State Army and the Kachin Independence Army, however, remain outstanding issues. As regional commanders continue to govern their areas unhampered by politicians at least until 2010, the patterns of relations established during the last two decades are now seemingly embedded; weaning them off their unfettered powers will not be easy.

The outward appearance of stasis within Myanmar, whatever the internal dynamics might be obscuring, will mean that condemnation of the regime by the United States and other Western governments, encouraged by exiled political activists, is likely to continue. However, after twenty years and a number of new factors emerging in the international balance of forces, one might expect to see a continued waning of the effectiveness of Western criticism. As the UN and regional organizations such as the Association of Southeast Asian Nations (ASEAN), South Asia Association for Regional Cooperation (SAARC) and Bay of Bengal Initiative for Multisectoral Technical Economic Cooperation (BIMSTEC) accept the road map and its implications, the establishment of normal relations between Myanmar and international financial institutions may be made possible after the 2010 elections. This would provide an impetus for genuine economic reform that would not only strengthen the regime but also civil society. Myanmar might then gradually shed its pariah image and begin to make up some of the lost years since the 1950s. Such a benign development would be welcomed by China and India, Myanmar's most important neighbours. International pressure will grow in the West to reconsider its position towards Myanmar following elections in 2010. Whether Myanmar can change its image, however, may be beyond the capacity of any government that is likely to come to power in Naypyitaw as the army will continue not merely to hold the ring, but to write and enforce the rules of the political game, for the foreseeable future.

Philippines

The Year 2009 does not promise much relief to Filipinos hoping to improve their quality of life. The wait has been a long one, spanning four decades and involving practically all political administrations. For 2009, the weak economy — characterized by fragile growth and persistent inequity and now sustained mostly by the remittances of a huge army of overseas Filipino workers — holds little promise of a revival any time soon. Reduced growth, increasing fiscal deficits, high inflation rates, much unemployment and even more underemployment will continue to challenge the country in 2009–10. A globalized world economy, which is currently in crisis mode, only increases the likelihood of a survivalist reading of the Philippine economy in the short term.

The political scenario is equally depressing. Beleaguered by recurring issues of feckless leadership, political illegitimacy, systemic corruption, pervasive politicking and gridlocked policy-making, the nation's governance has been acutely problematic. The situation is compounded by continuing communist and secessionist rebellions. Terrorist and brigand activity by the militant Abu Sayyaf and other lawless groups threaten the nation's security and the citizenry's public

PHILIPPINES

Land Area:	300,000 sq. km.
Population:	90.5 million (2008 estimate)
Capital:	Manila
Type of Government:	Presidential democracy
Head of State:	President Gloria Macapagal-Arroyo
Next Election:	May 2010
Currency Used:	Peso
US$ exchange rate on 18 November 2008:	US$1 = 49.7 peso

safety. Nothing on the horizon suggests that these governance challenges are soon to be mitigated despite optimistic pronouncements of publicly much-distrusted authorities. The sanguine vows of top civilian and military officials to end the communist insurgency in the next two years have little credibility. In the same fashion, few believe the Arroyo administration's assurances that peace talks with the Moro Islamic Liberation Front (MILF) will soon bring lasting peace to Mindanao.

Buffeted by the combined effects of economically difficult times and politically frustrating governance, most Filipinos face the immediate future with understandable trepidation. In a July 2008 national survey by Pulse Asia, 75 per cent of those polled said their quality of life deteriorated in the past year and nine in ten (88 per cent) expect it to remain the same or to worsen in 2009. One in five respondents would migrate to another country if possible. Given the national predicament, a small majority (56 per cent) manage to remain hopeful for the country but close to half (44 per cent) aver either indecision (29 per cent) or outright hopelessness (15 per cent). These views have persisted over the past five years and show little chance of improving in 2009–2010.

Despite worsening economic hardships and deepening political disillusionment, the Philippines in 2009–2010 will probably be unable to defer politics and, in its train, fractious politicking. The issue of the Arroyo administration's political legitimacy — triggered by the irregular transfer of power in 2001 from former President Joseph Estrada to his then Vice-President, now President Gloria Macapagal Arroyo, and compounded by the controversial 2004 presidential elections — has been a perennial focal point in the nation's politics. Four impeachment raps to date have been filed against President Arroyo. For many Filipinos, the President governs only with the support of the military and the police and she, it is often alleged, cannot risk alienating them. The large number of retired military and police officers in President Arroyo's cabinet and other influential agencies inclines many to believe that she is held captive by the national security establishment. Critics point out that she is forced to coddle senior military men charged with human rights violations and other criminal offenses.

Frequent scandals involving leading members of the administration have contributed a great deal to record levels of public disapproval and distrust for President Arroyo and most of her officials. The apparent inability or unwillingness of her administration to facilitate Senate inquiries into these scandals fuels a widespread sense of presidential stonewalling, probable personal involvement and, finally, political illegitimacy.

Precisely addressing the issue of presidential legitimacy, the elections of 2010 has become the central concern of Filipinos and their leaders. Whatever/whoever corrupted the presidential elections of 2004, most Filipinos are determined that they must now have credible elections where those who govern do not suffer a suspect mandate. President Arroyo's announcement that she will relinquish power in 2010 may not reassure many Filipinos that elections will definitely occur in 2010, but the political opposition and its fractious personalities have already stoked the nation's election fever. From as early as late 2007 and more so in 2008, opposition and administration presidential hopefuls have increasingly wooed the public with election-related messages and activities. The year 2009, and all the way to May 2010, will probably witness an election frenzy that brings out the worst in Philippine elections and its stakeholders. As before, massive, illegal diversion of public funds and unlawful intervention by critical public and private sector agencies, influential civilians and politicized men in uniform will probably take place. Oligarchic stakeholders — the dominant players in Philippine elections — usually treat elections as a no-holds-barred political contest. Their activities will be a major source of political instability in the Philippines in 2009–2010. In raiding the public treasury and worsening the already critical state of public finance, they necessarily foment violence and chaos in an ironic exercise seeking to gain legitimacy while employing illegitimate means.

Arrayed against these forces will be those interested in truly clean, democratic elections. Civil society groups that helped monitor elections in the past and a largely still marginalized, unorganized electorate will again pursue their democratic objectives. However, without investing enough in mass organizational work and confining themselves to a small elite and middle class constituency, their efforts to bring about democratic elections will probably be — as in the past — futile. A critical political lesson has yet to be learnt by struggling democrats in the Philippines; as even Machiavelli realized only too well, in politics those who do not build on the people build on foundations of sand.

Another scenario — one that aborts the 2010 elections through a willful use of charter change — is conceivable and some say is already in the works. It assumes that people cannot trust President Arroyo to keep a promise and, threatened by an imminent loss of political pre-eminence, she will do everything to stay in power. A formal structural change in governance — from presidential to parliamentary — could be railroaded by her allies in Congress to keep her in power as Prime Minister beyond 2010. Given the strong public opposition to charter change prior to the May 2010 elections, this deceptively legal scenario would also probably trigger much political destabilization.

When everything else fails, the final resort could be martial rule: elections are suspended, democratic forms are dispensed with and fully authoritarian governance ensues. Either Muslim secessionism or communist insurgency — with conveniently crafted supporting incidents — would be used to justify martial or emergency rule. Social engineering towards a seductive New Order might also be invoked as the global financial crisis is used to rationalize quick responses by leaders freed from presumably cumbersome democratic regulations.

In analysing short term political scenarios for the Philippines, one risks being suspected of suffering from paranoia, or at least unwarranted pessimism. The scenarios outlined here for 2009–2010 certainly exclude a comfortable reading of likely Philippine developments. Their realism, however, is precisely validated by the errors made by most analysts in forcing optimistic readings of the Philippines in 1972, upon the declaration of martial law by President Marcos, and again in 1986, when "people power" and "restored democracy" became the universal mantra of romantic analysts. For 2009–2010 as well, a more realistic assessment of the Philippine polity is called for and that reading unfortunately induces much apprehension among those who believe in democratic rule.

Singapore

For a multicultural society, Singapore has been surprisingly partial to homogeneity. The tiny urban landscape on which Singaporeans live has, for better or worse, made uniformity and standardization a necessity for bearable, efficient living. From public policies regarding mass housing to national service, the ideological aim has always been to unite the diverse, to homogenize the heterogeneous. And to a large extent, these national policies have succeeded, resulting in an ambiguous form of national identity and a well fenced comfort zone for the parochial.

Two announcements in 2008 carry the potential to interrupt the homogeneity in the political and social spheres in 2009 and beyond. The first came in the August National Day Rally Speech when Prime Minister Lee Hsien Loong announced that the ban on political films will be eased and that public protests would be allowed at Speakers Corner in Hong Lim Park. Previously, films or videos carrying political messages — the definition of which was often left to the discretion of civil servants — were banned under Section 33 of the Films Act. Prime Minister Lee said that the definition of a

SINGAPORE

Land Area:	692 sq. km.
Population:	4.84 million
Capital:	Singapore
Type of Government:	Parliamentary democracy
Head of State:	President S.R. Nathan
Prime Minister:	Lee Hsien Loong
Next Election:	By 2011
Currency Used:	Singapore Dollar
US$ exchange rate on 18 November 2008:	US$1 = S$1.52

"political film" would be narrowed, permitting more films to pass the censors. Outdoor public demonstrations at Speakers' Corner would be allowed as long as demonstrators adhered to existing rules and laws, and refrained from addressing issues related to race, language or religion. Since 1 September 2008, numerous applications have been submitted.

The second announcement, from the National Population Secretariat in September 2008, confirmed what anyone living in Singapore could not help but have noticed: Singapore's population spiked at 4.84 million in June 2008. This was a whopping 5.5 per cent increase, the largest annual population increase in the island's history. More pertinently, the number of foreigners increased by 19 per cent, Permanent Residents (PRs) by 6.5 per cent and citizens by a mere 1 per cent. Also interesting was the fact that an average of 950 Singaporeans gave up their citizenship each year to make their homes elsewhere.

There is little doubt that the first announcement was greeted with more relish than the second. Over the last few years, a coterie of amateur and overtly political film-makers, all blessed with varying degrees of talent, have emerged. These young film-makers, many of whom are sympathetic towards opposition politics, have spawned a body of work that offers an interesting, if not disjointed, documentation of local opposition figures, confrontations between civil society activists and the police and self-styled exposes of perceived authoritarianism.

With the easing of the political films ban, we can anticipate more of such films in 2009. We can expect to see more private or public screening of these non-mainstream films, more exposure on Youtube and widespread email distribution. Interestingly, many of these young film-makers do not profess any strong loyalty to a particular opposition party or figure, nor do they claim to be anti-government. Rather, their impetus comes from their strong belief that the mainstream government-controlled media, including the *Straits Times* and Mediacorp, do not adequately represent the diversity of politics in Singapore, often highlighting the opposition in a negative light, if at all. As such, it is from a sense of social justice and desire for parity that, rightly or wrongly, drives these film-makers on. And if their body of work grows bigger and more effective, not only will the political sphere become more lively and diverse in the coming years, these film-makers will also gain legitimacy as authentic voices from the ground in contrast to the state-guided one from mainstream media.

Political observers and academics will be watching to see how authorities handle such films as their circulation increases. As with most issues, it will not be the clear-cut cases that will garner the most interest but films that push the proverbial envelope such as those which may blend factual footage with heavy political biases to portray the government or the state in a poor light. The fate of such films will be the litmus test of the government's will to liberalize the political sphere.

The second announcement affects the everyday lives of Singaporeans more profoundly. The influx of foreigners has offered numerous anecdotal accounts of overcrowdedness on trains and buses, keen competition for jobs, fighting and drunkenness among foreign construction workers, fears for personal safety, language barriers between foreign service staff and local customers and so on.

Complaints aside, there may be more serious social consequences which could manifest themselves in 2009 and beyond. Firstly, and broadly speaking, it is clear that a section of Singaporeans are uneasy over the influx of new faces and accents. This uneasiness surfaced in protests from the residents of Serangoon Gardens, a middle class suburban estate, against plans to build a dormitory for foreign workers. The fact that some of these residents argued that crime rates would go up, despite the fact that there is no correlation between criminality and increased levels of immigration, demonstrates the readiness to demonize these workers when they enter the personal spaces of citizens.

Secondly, non-Chinese Singaporeans are already raising concerns over the undeniable increase of staff from the People's Republic of China (PRC) in the local service industry. Many Malay, Indian and even English-educated Chinese Singaporeans are frustrated that these PRC staff do not speak English. These woes add to the feeling that the sensitivities of ethnic minorities in Singapore are often overlooked. The crux of the issue is the balance between market logic, which shows that these Mandarin-speaking PRC service staff do cater to the local Chinese majority, and the political will of the government to intervene and make rudimentary English lessons mandatory if only as a symbolic gesture to the multicultural complexion of Singapore.

Thirdly, there are also more PRs and new citizens. In the first half of 2008, 34,800 were granted PR status, up by some 20 per cent from the same period in 2007. Meanwhile, 9,600 were granted citizenship, up by some 30 per cent, compared to the year before. And nearly 7 in 10 new PRs aged 20 and above had post-secondary qualifications. The integration of these PRs and new citizens who bring with them their own national and civic experiences from their countries of origin with those of Singaporeans born and bred here will be a major challenge. Integration is going to be more elusive in a cosmopolitan society when PRs and new citizens find that they have more in common with other foreigners and expatriates than Singaporeans who have undergone collective experiences like national service or the local education system. This has given rise to fears that idea and memory of Singapore, and what it means to be Singaporean, is going to change too much for the comfort of some.

These two announcements, more than most, will inject diversity into Singapore life in the coming year. Such diversities are accoutrements of the country's global city function and represent a challenge to the young nation. As the city-state oscillates between the needs of a nation and the demands of the global city, the homogeneity in the different areas of Singapore life will be threatened, resulting in still unfolding consequences.

Thailand

Despite the restoration of representative government following the December 2007 elections, political stability in Thailand in 2009–2010 will remain elusive.

Beginning in May 2008, the predominantly right-wing anti-government movement known as the People's Alliance for Democracy (PAD) staged extended protests against the coalition government led by the People's Power Party (PPP). The PPP is effectively a rebranded version of Thai Rak Thai (TRT), the Thaksin-led party that was dissolved by the Constitutional Tribunal after the 2006 military coup. The PPP stands accused by the PAD of being a proxy for Thaksin, and of plotting to replace the 2007 constitution — drafted by a military-appointed assembly — with a reincarnation of the 1997 constitution.

The PAD originally ignited the anti-Thaksin movement in 2006 with corruption allegations against the Prime Minister. Their protests contributed to the military coup, which in turn escalated conflict among civil society, polarized political constituencies, and led to the ongoing crisis of constitutional monarchy and the rule of law in Thailand. The 2008 revival of the PAD was provoked by a range of conservative and nationalist agendas, including a fierce dispute over the Preah Vihear temple on the Thai-Cambodian border. In September 2008, Prime Minister Samak Sundaravej was forced to resign by the

THAILAND

Land Area:	514,000 sq. km.
Population:	65 million
Capital:	Bangkok
Type of Government:	Parliamentary democracy, with constitutional monarch
Head of State:	King Bhumibol Adulyadej
Prime Minister:	Somchai Wongsawat
Next Election:	By December 2011
Currency Used:	Baht
US$ exchange rate on 18 November 2008:	US$1 = 35.24 baht

courts, paving the way for the installation of Thaksin's brother-in-law, Somchai Wongsawat, as Prime Minister.

The PPP itself stands accused of committing election fraud and is very likely to be dissolved by the courts. But this time they are ready: PPP members have already set up a new political party, known as Puea Thai (For Thai), which they plan to join if the PPP is dissolved. Judicial institutions are still playing a significant role in the political crisis, which has called into question their neutrality.

Given the current situation, predicting the political outlook for 2009 is fraught with difficulties. There is a high possibility that parliament will be dissolved and that a general election will be held in late 2008 or early 2009. Blood has already been shed in riots outside parliament on 7 October 2008, which saw two PAD protestors killed and more than 400 people injured. Further violence could bring matters to a head, and the possibility of another military coup cannot be ruled out.

The ongoing conflict goes far beyond standard conflicts between government and opposition parties, but represents sustained efforts to challenge parliamentary democracy itself. The PAD has asserted that western-style liberal democracy is unsuitable for Thailand, and that a "new politics" should be explored, one no longer reliant on the principle of one person, one voter. PAD leaders have criticized uneducated rural voters as a root cause of the current political crisis. One PAD proposal has even suggested a 70:30 formula: popular representatives should be 70 per cent nominated by certain occupational groups and 30 per cent elected. While this formula does not represent a worked-out proposal, it indicates the broad thrust of the PAD's platform, one supported by a range of intellectuals and other influential actors.

While elected politicians and their allies are bound to resist such proposals, it seems that 2009 will be dominated by attempts to negotiate the emerging discourse of "new politics", which both revisits and yet differs from the 1990s discourse of "political reform". Thai society is currently walking a tightrope due to deep divisions between two groups, divisions which cut across elite, military, bureaucratic and business networks and involve actors such as doctors, state enterprise unions, students, activists, the media and grassroots movements. The first group, broadly aligned with the PAD, claims to be acting in defence of "nation, religion and monarchy". The PAD gained momentum by reproducing the discourse of "saving the nation"; PAD supporters believe that Thaksin and his proxies are threatening the three core pillars of Thai identity. The second group argues that legitimate power can only be based on elections, popular representation and parliamentary democracy.

Between these two groups lies a large silent majority who feel confused and frustrated by the continuing conflict and are hoping for a quick end to the impasse. It seems likely that this silent majority will ultimately acquiesce to some version of "new politics", if promoted by the conservative elite as a reformist solution, and one that appears to offer an end to instability. 2009–2010 is likely to be a period of further constitutional change or transformation of political structures. Because of anxieties about the royal succession and the involvement of certain elites in post-succession scenarios, the stakes in this political struggle are extremely high. While there is no firm evidence to link the Palace with the ongoing conflict, both sides are gradually beginning to perceive connections, a view which is also spreading to the general public. The result is a symbolic war between colour-coded camps: a deep confrontation between red (pro-Thaksin) and yellow (pro-monarchy).

Groups on the red side have made highly critical comments concerning the Privy Council and monarchy, despite the existence of strict lèse-majesté laws, which may be strongly challenged in 2009. A number of lèse-majesté cases have recently been brought against both Thai and non-Thai defendants. The intense social conflict has politicized debate concerning the role of the monarchy as never before in recent Thai history. The mainstream media employs institutionalized censorship to curtail these debates, but they have now migrated into cyberspace, where the authorities have begun blocking websites on grounds of lèse-majesté. The Internet offers a new dimension for Thai social and political life, one that looks set to assume ever-greater importance despite the vigorous attempts of the Criminal Court and other agencies to prevent open discussion of sensitive topics. In the ongoing government-versus-PAD stand-off, both sides have utilized the electronic media both to mobilize hatred and to build social consensus.

International pressure will remain a key factor in deterring the military from staging another coup. Yet the global economic downturn may yet have some direct ramifications in Thailand, just as the 1997 Asian Financial Crisis was a catalyst for rethinking the political direction of the country. Faced with a range of economic, political and social problems, Thai people are largely pessimistic about the future, and are increasingly turning to religion for answers. Social problems are growing, while political conflicts in Bangkok divert media and government attention away from marginalized groups. The medium term outlook suggests that serious social issues will remain neglected until Thailand can redefine its sense of national political direction. The same applies to the insurgency in the Deep South; serious proposals regarding a political solution have not been seriously addressed as national politics have taken priority. There are parallels between violence and resistance at the national and local levels; when Bangkok is in turmoil, rebellion in the southern border provinces is likely to fester.

Under these circumstances, the political temperature will remain feverish for much of 2009. Many Thai citizens are deeply engaged politically, but the very future of parliamentary democracy has been called into question. Because tensions have reached such levels, national reconciliation now seems a very idealistic notion.

Vietnam

In *Regional Outlook 2008–2009* it was pointed out that some political turbulence in Vietnam was to be expected at the end of 2008. Indeed, throughout 2008 the political chatter centered on the agenda of the Central Committee of the Vietnamese Communist Party's (VCP) meeting due to be held in early 2009. In particular, the early retirement of the current General Secretary, Nong Duc Manh, has been much discussed, although officially this item is not on the agenda yet and there are no obvious signs that his powerbase has been weakened. This demonstrates that the intra-party debate on whether there should be a change of leadership mid-term is far from over. The change of leadership rumour is unlikely to go away, which merely confirms the desire for stronger and more decisive leadership among Vietnamese who want to see a faster pace of reform than that achieved under Nong Duc Manh.

Three main currents are likely to influence political developments in 2009–2010. Firstly, the Central Committee meeting of 2009 is now likely to become the mid-term plenary of the VCP. A mid-term plenary serves as an opportunity to review the party's performance over the past thirty months. Undoubtedly at the plenary there will also be attempts to review the performances of the country's leaders, and for them to accept responsibility, or even step down. The current set of leaders is steering the ship of state through a global economic crisis, whose severe impact on Vietnam is due in large part to the lack of effective leadership in economic policy. The pace of implementing structural reforms needed to take Vietnam to the next level of economic growth is widely considered to have slowed down considerably, and senior party members who want faster change point the finger of blame at the General Secretary.

VIETNAM

Land area:	332,000 sq. km.
Population:	86.2 million
Capital:	Hanoi
Type of Government:	Socialist Republic
Head of State:	President Nguyen Minh Triet
General Secretary of the Vietnamese Communist Party:	Nguyen Duc Manh
Prime Minister:	Nguyen Tan Dung
Next Election:	2011
Currency Used:	Dong
US$ exchange rate on 18 November 2008:	US$1 = 17,272 dong

Other signs, however, show that Nong Duc Manh is still very much in charge: he is still the chairperson of the personnel committee that will prepare leadership changes for the 11th Party Congress, and he is still responsible for drafting important documents for that event. Yet, it is clear that party unity and the moral authority of the party's top leadership have taken something of a hit, not just because of economic problems, but also over the brouhaha of the PMU18 scandal. Corruption charges against Nguyen Viet Tien, the ex-Vice Minister for Transport, were dropped. He was also going to be given back his old position before he was suspended because of the corruption charges. But his victory was short-lived: not too long after a party directive relieved him of his government job and dismissed him from all party positions. These contradictory moves and lack of coherence confounded many Vietnamese, and left few in doubt that a political struggle was taking place. As the 2011 Congress approaches, we can expect further struggles to be conducted in proxy over corruption scandals.

The second current is the preparations for the 11th Party Congress in 2011. The Congress lays out policy and makes key leadership changes to achieve the desired policy impact. From 2009 until the Congress takes place, academics and policy analysts of the Party and the government will dissect the country's progress over the past thirty months, debate them in terms of the Party's policy platforms and then recommend to the Party leadership goals for the next five years. In this regard we could see continuing political tensions over several questions that have not been settled. These include matters of equitization of state enterprises (corporatizing them and selling shares to employees) and the control of huge state conglomerates. Key issues of governance, especially in the provision of fundamental public services, such as education and health, remain key challenges that do not necessarily have easy answers. Administrative reforms to reduce the size of the government still face significant resistance from bureaucrats who oppose outsourcing non-policy work. While the economy is much more robust and integrated with the world than a decade ago, politics and governance are still very much command systems in nature.

The third current is how quickly Vietnam recovers its footing and draws up measures to advance economic development. The country was only lightly affected by the global financial crisis in the third quarter of 2008, but perhaps only because it had had its own financial crisis two quarters earlier and by the end of the year the government had learnt some important lessons about macroeconomic management. Nevertheless, given that export markets in the United States and Europe are key to its growth strategy, Vietnam is likely to suffer a downturn in exports. The political legitimacy of the VCP has depended to a large extent on economic growth and political stability. Economic problems strike at the very core of that legitimacy, and at such times corruption within the government will be looked upon less kindly by people than when the economy was booming.

We should no doubt expect the government to do its utmost to restore the confidence levels Vietnam enjoyed in 2007. More importantly, it is hoped that the government will use the current economic crisis as an opportunity to carry out further structural reforms in order to meet the challenge of competition from other transitional countries, not to mention the economic juggernauts of China and India. The government will also need to deal effectively with other important issues such as the provision of education, creating a skilled workforce, health care and infrastructure bottlenecks in Hanoi and Ho Chi Minh City. In the run-up to the 11ᵗʰ Party Congress, the leadership should avoid tying itself into knots with esoteric ideological debates about "market economy with socialist orientations". At a time when credit is tight and global recession looms, Vietnam should focus on increasing foreign and domestic investment, and expanding exports than on trying to reconcile globalization with the communist ideology. Theoreticians should "take five".

ECONOMIC OUTLOOK

REGIONAL ECONOMIC OUTLOOK

By Sanchita Basu Das and Omkar Lal Shrestha

Southeast Asia will face a slowdown in its economic growth at least over the next one year. In 2008, the region's economic growth is expected to moderate around 5.4 per cent (Asian Development Outlook (ADO) 2008), sliding further in the first half of 2009. This is significantly slower than the 6.5 per cent growth achieved in 2007. Going into 2010, the economies are predicted to experience a modest growth recovery. Depending on how long and how severe the global financial crisis will be, there is downside risks to the forecast estimates.

The growth prospect for Southeast Asia is especially deteriorating because the region still depends on the G3 economies (United States, Euro-zone and Japan) for its economic business cycle. The U.S. economy grew by almost 2 per cent in the first half of 2008, with the downside risk steadily increasing for the next six months. The negative spillover effect from the already strained financial market is pressing the risk factor, worsening the growth expectation. This is likely to downgrade

---

REGIONAL ECONOMIC OUTLOOK

- In 2008–2009, Southeast Asia's economic growth will taper off to 5.0–5.5 per cent from a high of 6.5 per cent in 2007.

- High base effect and anti-inflationary measures are expected to bring down the inflation in 2009.

- Under the weight of subsidies for food and fuel, fiscal positions are at risk.

- External positions are stronger for primary commodity exporters.

the growth for Europe and Japan going into 2009 (see Table 1). Slower exports to the G3 economies will lead to gradual decrease in domestic demand and hence lower profit margins and investment in the Asian private sector. The fiscal spending may ameliorate some of the slowdown but it would not be enough to alter the entire growth dynamics for the region. The growth would also hinge on the quick resolution of the ongoing global financial stress.

The growth in the region is also dampened by the increased concern about the global financial outlook and investors' declining investment appetite. The stock markets faced panic selling reflecting the sentiments of the U.S. market. These kind of large swings are bound to influence consumers' and investors' confidence, thus dragging down the contagion impact on the domestic economies.

For Southeast Asia, 2008 is also a year of sharp increases in fuel and food prices. While the international oil price peaked to US$140 per barrel, the rice price soared from US$372 in end 2007 to more than US$500 per metric ton during 2008. This had a varied impact among the countries, depending on their economic state, their dependence on imports of these products and available policy options. For example, in the Philippines, Singapore and Thailand, domestic oil prices are deregulated and determined by market forces. Hence domestic fuel prices mirrored the rising international oil prices. However, for Malaysia

Table 1: Global and Asian GDP Outlook

	2006	2007	2008f	2009f
Industrial Countries*	2.7	2.2	1.3	1.1
U.S.	2.8	2.0	1.3	1.0
EU	2.8	2.6	1.4	1.4
Japan	2.4	2.1	1.0	1.0
China	11.7	11.9	10.0	9.5
India	9.6	9.0	7.4	7.0
Southeast Asia	6.0	6.5	5.4	5.4

NOTE: *Growth rates for industrial countries are a GDP-weighted average for the U.S., Euro-zone and Japan.
SOURCE: Asian Development Bank.

and Indonesia the governments partially subsidize high oil prices. With regards to food prices too, the regional picture is diverse. While for exporters (like Thailand), international increases in prices are fast reflected in domestic prices; for importers (such as the Philippines), the pass-through to domestic rice prices tends to be incomplete given the country's public distribution system.

The overall inflation in the region has accelerated at a faster pace than expected. According to ADB outlook, the 2008 full year inflation would be around 9.4 per cent (*vis-à-vis* 4.0 per cent in 2007), before pulling back to 6.9 per cent in 2009. The inflation shock is likely to dissipate for most of the economies in the region. This is due to favourable base effects and declining food and energy prices. These effects are expected to spread region wide through 2009. The slowdown in Asia and the global economy are expected to further bring down Asian inflation. All this would create some room for policy flexibility

Figure 1: Real GDP Growth in the ASEAN-5 Countries, 2003–2009

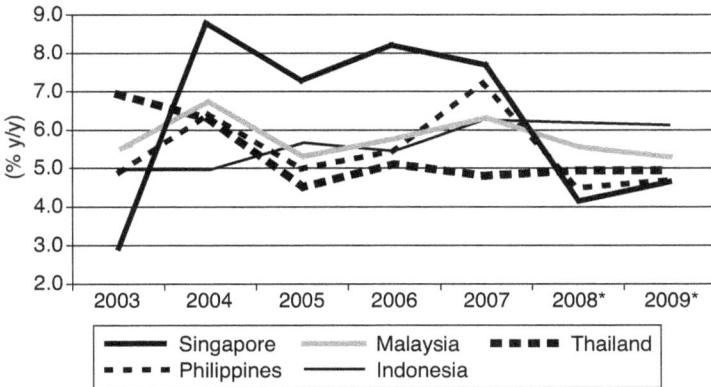

NOTE: * Estimated GDP growth rates for 2008 and 2009.
SOURCE: Asian Development Bank (estimates are as of ADO update, September 2008).

for the Central Banks in future. Earlier in 2008, monetary policy has been tightened in most of the larger countries (except Malaysia) on accelerating inflationary pressure with the most severe in Vietnam, followed by Indonesia, the Philippines and Thailand.

In addition to inflation, rising food and fuel prices had serious fiscal implications. It was particularly worrisome for countries providing direct subsidies like Indonesia and Malaysia. Although these two countries attempted for lowering subsidy to contain fiscal deficit, funds have been reallocated as assistance to the poor. Elsewhere, while Vietnam tightened its fiscal policy to reduce demand side pressure on inflation, Singapore marked another year of large surplus.

With the sharper than anticipated deterioration in global growth environment and the expected lower exports, the terms-of-trade is also likely to be weaker for Southeast Asia. The external current account surplus as a share of regional GDP is projected at 4.7 per cent in

Figure 2: Real GDP Growth in Cambodia, Laos, Vietnam and Southeast Asia, 2003–2009

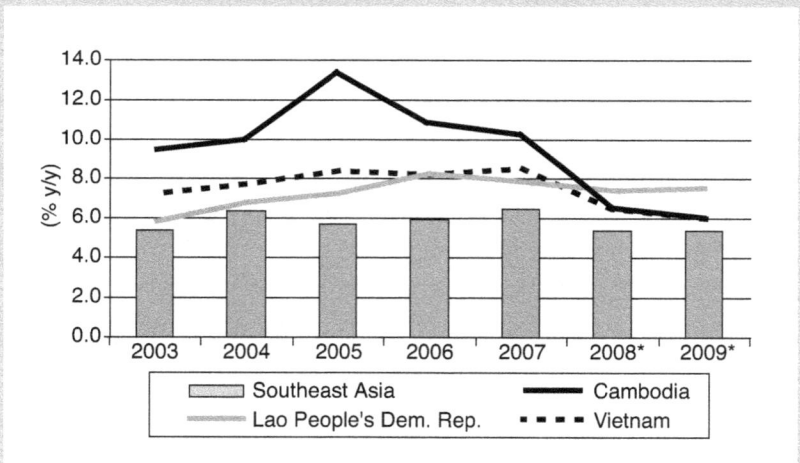

NOTE: * Estimated GDP growth rates for 2008 and 2009.
SOURCE: Asian Development Bank, see Figure 1.

2008, down from 7.4 per cent in 2007 (ADO 2008). This could improve slightly to 5.1 per cent going into 2009. However, individually, the country's performance will differ. The surpluses would be narrower for Indonesia and Thailand because of strong domestic demand as well as higher costs of oil imports for the latter. Vietnam's deficit is projected to widen as its imports rose on expectation of dong devaluation. In contrast, the surplus is expected to be larger in case of Malaysia on higher commodity prices.

On the whole, moving into 2009–2010, growth momentum in Southeast Asia will depend much on global growth expectation and the path of regional fiscal stimulus (supportive to domestic demand). Although Asia is not as reliant on the U.S. as earlier, this does not mean complete decoupling. About 15–20 per cent of Asia's exports still head for the U.S. economy. The ADB, in its 2008 outlook, showed there is a clear link between retail sales in the U.S. and Asian exports. Hence,

Figure 3: Inflation Rate in Southeast Asian Economies, 2007–2009

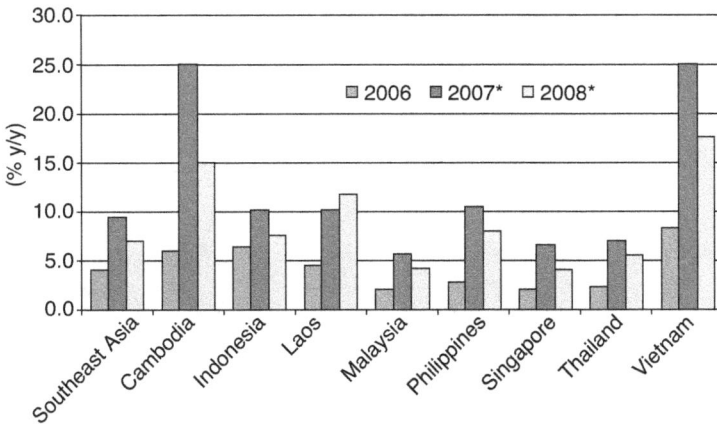

NOTE: * Estimated inflation rates for 2008 and 2009.
SOURCE: Asian Development Bank, see Figure 1.

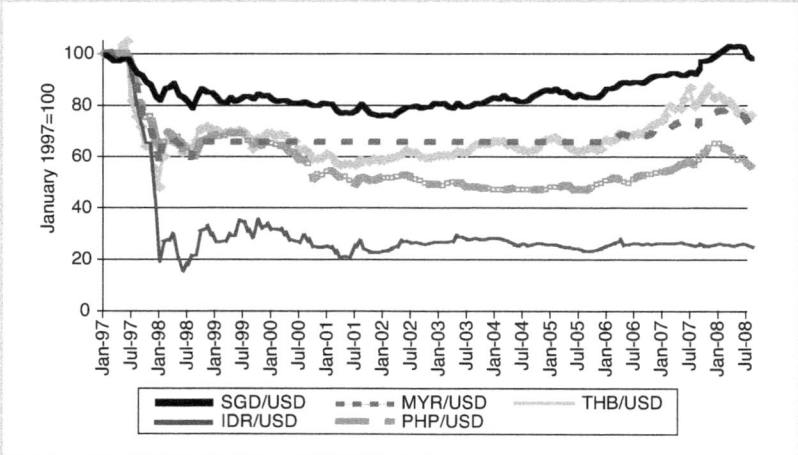

Figure 4: Relative Performance of ASEAN-5 Currencies to the U.S. Dollar, 1997–2008

SOURCE: Bloomberg.

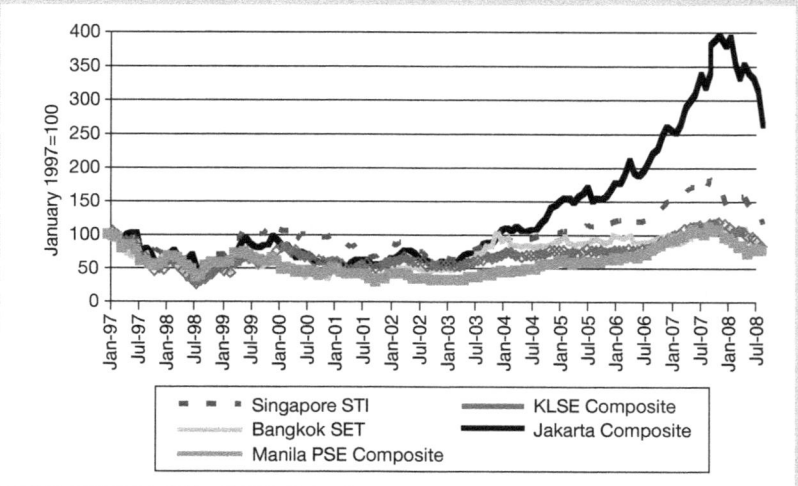

Figure 5: Relative Performance of ASEAN-5 Main Stockmarket Indices, 1997–2008

SOURCE: Bloomberg.

any retrenchment of U.S. consumer spending will take a bite from Asia's export story. Overtime, Asian economies will need to learn to manage growth from other factors — higher domestic demand and investment. This can partially offset the slowdown from the global recession.

REFERENCES

Asian Development Bank. *Asian Development Outlook Update, September 2008*.

——. *Asian Development Outlook, April 2008*.

THE WORLD TRADING SYSTEM AND SOUTHEAST ASIA: EMERGING PROTECTIONISM AND POST-DOHA CHALLENGES
By Razeen Sally

The World Trade Organisation's Doha Round has collapsed, perhaps terminally. This predictable failure reflects a much deeper malaise. Policies governing international trade and investment have become hopelessly outdated. They are stuck in anachronistic twentieth-century mindsets, institutions and regulations, increasingly disconnected from today's business realities. WTO malfunction is symptomatic, but so is the profusion of commercially nonsensical preferential trade agreements (PTAs). These policy fault lines are found as much in the ASEAN countries as elsewhere. Overall, trade policy in ASEAN and elsewhere in Asia has swung within a decade from non-discriminatory unilateral and multilateral liberalisation to discriminatory PTAs.

Why is trade policy in the region not up to the challenge of containing emerging protectionist threats and launching a fresh wave of market reforms? And what must be changed to make policy relevant to real-world producers and consumers, and enable rather than hinder twenty-first century globalization?

- Trade policies around the world have become disconnected from business and consumer realities. They are not up to the challenges of twenty-first century globalization. That also applies to Southeast Asia.

- The Doha Round is commercially largely irrelevant. What matters is the WTO post-Doha. Above all, multilateral trade rules need to be protected and strengthened. That requires "coalitions of the willing" among capable and willing governments.

- So-called FTAs in Asia — including those of the ASEAN countries — are "trade light" and cause business complications with their multiple discriminatory provisions. They make little sense in a twenty-first century world of global supply chains. That also applies to regional economic integration initiatives such as ASEAN+3 and ASEAN+6.

- Creeping protectionism is likely to accelerate with the end of the Goldilocks global economy and the onset of financial crisis. This will be dangerous and costly — not least for Southeast Asian countries which are so dependent on global markets.

- The key to revive stalled trade and investment reforms in the region is unilateral liberalization and competitive emulation, not trade negotiations. Trade reforms, especially to tackle domestic regulatory barriers, should be hitched to domestic reform agendas.

First, any meaningful trade reforms must address the trade problems of today. Some concern familiar protectionist instruments such as tariffs, quotas, trade-distorting subsidies and anti-dumping duties. More damagingly, protectionism appears increasingly in the guise of opaque non-tariff regulatory barriers and onerous restrictions on foreign direct investment (FDI), not least in key services sectors. These "trade-related" barriers keep business costs high. They prevent countries from reaping the full benefits of globalization and spreading them widely at home. "Second-generation" reforms are sorely needed to tear down these anti-competitive walls, but they have hardly materialized. This picture is reflected in most ASEAN countries' poor scores in the World Bank's "ease of doing business" rankings.

Second, the Doha Round should be finished as soon as possible, or else scrapped. What was on the table was so full of exemptions, flexibilities, escape clauses and implementation conditions that only the Geneva circuit of trade negotiators, academics and NGO junkies could understand the details. Endlessly pursuing a midget, largely commercially irrelevant deal is not worth the candle.

Attention should now switch to a post-Doha agenda. Above all, the latter should shift emphasis from *liberalization to rules*. Sadly, substantial multilateral liberalization is highly unlikely. It is arguably more important to close loopholes, safeguard the principle of non-discrimination, make trade procedures more transparent and user-friendly, and generally update vital multilateral rules for stable and open international commerce.

This presupposes a more differentiated WTO. The reality outside Geneva is that the OECD plus about twenty advanced developing countries account for about 90 per cent of world trade and FDI. This includes the more developed ASEAN countries. Within this outer core there is an inner core of Big Beasts: the USA, EU, and now China, India and Brazil. These outer and inner cores should come together in self-selecting "coalitions of the willing" to sign up to stronger rules. That should include ASEAN countries that are both capable and willing — Singapore certainly, Malaysia and Thailand probably, Indonesia and Philippines maybe, plus fast-globalizing Vietnam. Finally, the WTO should adapt to a more modest, politically realistic future. That means an end to big trade

THE WORLD TRADING SYSTEM AND SOUTHEAST ASIA (continued)

rounds with high ambitions and expectations.

Third, all sorts of discriminatory trade deals need a serious rethink. PTAs have spread like wildfire. Over 200 are in force, with many more on the way. According to the ADB, nearly 40 PTAs have been concluded in East Asia, with over 60 other initiatives in the pipeline. Nearly all are "trade light". They carve out politically sensitive sectors as well as crucial rules (e.g. on anti-dumping duties and agricultural subsidies). They barely advance on weak WTO disciplines on domestic regulatory barriers. They deliver little, if any, net liberalization. Finally, they get tied up in knots of restrictive regulations on rules of origin, tariff schedules, services and investment. This makes no sense in a twenty-first century world of spliced-up cross-border production networks brought together in complex global supply chains. Companies plugged into global supply chains need simple, transparent, non-discriminatory rules, not spaghetti bowls that add to red tape and increase business costs.

With the possible exception of some of Singapore's PTAs (notably the U.S.-Singapore FTA), all bilateral PTAs between ASEAN countries and third countries are trade-light, as are collective ASEAN PTAs with China, India, Japan and South Korea. At best they eliminate tariffs on 90 per cent or more of existing trade. But that in itself creates little extra trade given relatively low tariffs on most goods and restrictive rules of origin on sensitive products. Worse, these PTAs hardly make a dent into trade-related regulatory barriers in services, investment, government procurement and so on. That is where the real potential gains lie. This reflects the picture within ASEAN: the ASEAN Free Trade Area looks good on tariff elimination (which hardly makes any difference), but avoids tackling the regulatory barriers that count.

The new conventional wisdom is that region-wide PTAs, such as ASEAN+3 and ASEAN+6, are the answer. These initiatives are open doors to shallow conferencitis — another policy dead-end. Intra-Asian political and economic divisions will prevent strong agreements from emerging: they are likely to be as trade-light as current bilateral PTAs. They will also add extra layers of discriminatory regulation. And they will distract attention from the core business of domestic structural reforms.

Fourth, it is imperative that the engine of autonomous trade liberalization does not stall. Future global market reforms depend on it. Most recent trade and FDI liberalization has not come from the WTO and PTAs but from governments taking down barriers *unilaterally*, outside trade negotiations. In fact this accounts for two-thirds of developing-country tariff liberalization since the early 1980s.

Nowhere has unilateral liberalization been stronger than in East and Southeast Asia. That is how countries in the region inserted themselves into global supply chains. China followed from the early 1990s, and in turn induced similiar liberalization elsewhere in the region.

Fifth, there are several emerging protectionist threats, now more dangerous with the end of the Goldilocks world economy, the onset of global financial crisis and a probable slowdown in growth. Reregulation of financial markets threatens to spill over into extra protectionism in other services sectors, and beyond into manufacturing. Creeping protectionism, already visible before the global credit crunch, will likely accelerate. There will be a stronger backlash in the West and in other developing countries against China's and India's advancing global economic integration — accompanied perhaps by stalled reforms in China and India, and indeed in the ASEAN countries, for a prolonged period. There will continue to be widespread resistance to migration, and more generally to people crossing borders in search of work. Investment and energy nationalism are on the rise — notably increasing FDI restrictions in "strategic" sectors. Price and trade controls are being used to combat food and fuel inflation. And initiatives in Europe and America to combat climate change are set to become the new Trojan Horse of protectionism.

These measures, if not contained, will slow down globalization's advance and its spread of benefits. Worse, creeping protectionism threatens to get out of hand and unravel the historic market reforms of the 1980s and 1990s. That would signal a retreat to the 1970s, which saw a disastrous combination of domestic market restrictions, beggar-thy-neighbour protectionism and stagflation.

Trade policy in Southeast Asia must become less of a foreign-policy plaything in remote, lumbering international institutions. Instead, it should be hitched to domestic economic policy and its institutional framework. It has to be grounded in *domestic* reforms, especially on the trade-related regulatory barriers that constitute a second-generation reform agenda. It has to be reconnected to bread-and-butter realities for business and consumers. This is essentially a matter of unilateral action and competitive emulation among governments. A revitalized, businesslike, post-Doha WTO should assist such reforms with stronger multilateral rules that protect the world trading system from a noxious combination of discriminatory bilateral and regional deals and emerging protectionism.

APEC AT 20: RETROSPECT AND PROSPECT
By Melanie S. Milo

The year 2009 marks the 20th anniversary of the first APEC ministerial meeting in Canberra. Singapore will also take its turn to host APEC for the second time in 2009, and its first time to host an APEC Economic Leaders Meeting (AELM). Singapore first hosted APEC in 1990, when it was still a ministerial-level consultative meeting. To say that things are different twenty years hence, both with respect to APEC itself and the environment in which it operates, would be an understatement.

Retrospect[1]

APEC started as an informal ministerial level dialogue group of twelve economies formed at the November 1989 meeting in Canberra (see Table 1). Four inter-related factors have been identified to explain why APEC was finally established when much earlier attempts failed: (i) increasing trade and investment in the Asia-Pacific region; (ii) common interest in an open international trading regime; (iii) growing concerns about regional trading arrangements elsewhere in the world, particularly the possible rise of a fortress Europe; and (iv) trade disputes among APEC members, particularly those involving China, Japan, and the U.S. (Janow 1997).

Australia, which spearheaded the initiative together with Japan, initially proposed a very specific agenda for the group — to become a mini-OECD in the Asia-Pacific region. But that proposal was not adopted at the initial meeting, which was more exploratory in nature in terms of identifying the group's agenda. The primary statement made was the group's expression of full support for trade liberalization, particularly the successful completion of the Uruguay Round of the GATT which was in its 3rd year of negotiations at that time. The three ministerial meetings that followed likewise endorsed the successful completion of the Uruguay Round.

It was only at the 1991 meeting in Seoul that APEC identified key operating principles for the group, which included: "to sustain the growth and development of the region...; to enhance the positive gains resulting from increasing economic

---

[1] This section draws heavily on various documents, publications, and other materials available on the APEC website <www.apec.org>.

inter-dependence...; to develop and strengthen the open multilateral trading system...; to reduce barriers to trade in goods and services and investment among participants." Finally, it was agreed to formalize the APEC process through annual ministerial meetings supplemented by meetings of senior officials, and the establishment of working groups to undertake the work programmes (Janow 1997).

Developing a vision for trade for the group up to the year 2000 was then delegated to the Eminent Persons Group (EPG), which the ministers agreed to establish at the 1992 meeting in Bangkok. The ministers also agreed to establish a small secretariat in Singapore to provide administrative support.

The first EPG report came out in October 1993 and outlined a four-part strategy to "create a genuine Asia Pacific Economic Community" over time: (i) a goal of free trade in the Asia Pacific; (ii) trade facilitation programme; (iii) technical assistance programme; and (iv) modest institutionalization of APEC. The first three were subsequently referred to as the three pillars of APEC's work programme. On trade liberalization, it endorsed the successful completion of the Uruguay Round by the end of 1993 and encouraged APEC members to call for the launch of the next major global negotiation by the end of 1995. It also called on APEC members to agree to reach agreement in 1996 on a target date and timetable for the achievement of free trade in the region (EPG 1993).

After a slow start, the group gained significant traction when the U.S., as APEC host economy, convened the first APEC Economic Leaders' Meeting (AELM) in November 1993. The meeting was opportune because it took place less than a month before the deadline of the conclusion of the Uruguay Round. Although the EPG's recommendation of setting a timetable for the achievement of free trade in the region was not adopted either by the leaders or the ministers, the APEC Leaders Economic Vision Statement referred to "a community of Asia Pacific economies". The leaders also asked EPG to develop more concrete proposals on how to achieve the long term goal of free trade in the region. The ministers again issued a declaration on the Uruguay Round, but this time offering additional tariff concessions from APEC members (Janow 1997). The APEC meetings in Seattle, most notably the first AELM which represented a strong show of regional commitment and solidarity, have been credited as making a major contribution to the conclusion of the Uruguay Round in April 1994. The argument was that

APEC AT 20: RETROSPECT AND PROSPECT (continued)

the prospect of APEC moving ahead on an agenda of regional trade liberalization forced the EU to make some concessions.

The second EPG report came out in August 1994. The report first identified key operating principles that underpinned it: free trade and investment; international cooperation; regional solidarity; mutual benefit; mutual respect and egalitarianism; pragmatism; decision making on the basis of consensus, implementation on the basis of flexibility; and open regionalism. Based on these principles, the report recommended the immediate adoption of a comprehensive programme to achieve the long term goal of "free and open trade and investment in the region". The timetable proposed was to complete the programme of trade liberalization by 2000 and complete liberalization by 2020, with the economically advanced members taking the lead. The third and final report of the EPG released in 1995 focused on the implementation of the proposed APEC vision.

In the 1994 Bogor Declaration, APEC leaders agreed to adopt the EPG recommendation, and set free and open trade and investment by 2010 for industrialized economies and 2020 for developing economies as the long term goal of the APEC process. To operationalize the Bogor goals, the Osaka Action Agenda (OAA) was drafted in 1995 as a roadmap, which identified the principles and areas for trade and investment liberalization and facilitation, together with the elements and areas for technical cooperation. And in 1996, Individual Action Plans (IAPs) and the Collective Action Plan (CAP), together referred to as the Manila Action Plan for APEC (MAPA), were drawn up to further concretize moves towards the Bogor goals.

The principle of "open regionalism" meant that APEC initiatives would be consistent with multilateral rules. The OAA went further by endorsing the acceleration of Uruguay Round commitments, which was reflected in most of the IAPs. The unequivocal language in which the Bogor Declaration was crafted meant that the ultimate measure of APEC's success in trade and investment liberalization was whether the implementation of the IAPs and CAP would truly produce significant results in terms of strengthening global trade and investment liberalization (Janow 1997).

The year 1997 was designated as APEC's Year of Action, and marked the first year of implementation of the IAPs. However, the Asian financial crisis that broke out in April 1997 was a serious disruption to what has been a period of strong economic growth for the region. Simply put, APEC was severely criticized for failing to provide any significant response to help the economies directly involved in the crisis, which were all APEC member economies. This despite the inclusion of the APEC Finance Ministers Meeting in the APEC process in 1994. The 1997 Leaders Declaration in Vancouver did not even outrightly use the term "financial crisis". It only emphasized the role of the IMF in responding to such crisis, while relegating APEC's role to dialogue and cooperation with the multilateral agencies in reforming financial systems. There was no mention of its possible role in the bailout of the affected member economies. In particular, the U.S. did not play a significant role the way it did in the mid-1990s Mexican bailout.

Instead, the leaders affirmed their commitment to trade and investment liberalization, and endorsed the ministers' proposal to fast track the early voluntary sectoral liberalization (EVSL) programme. However, strong opposition to the EVSL by Japan and the other Asian member economies led to its abandonment. Simply put, the focus on the EVSL at the height of the Asian crisis was ill-timed, even misguided. The two events were seen as significant failures on the part of APEC, and marked the weakening of APEC's influence and relevance in the region and hence the rest of the world.

According to Ravenhill (2006), "the EVSL debacle effectively removed trade liberalization from the APEC agenda" (p. 11), although APEC would continue to make pronouncements in support of the WTO and the Doha Development Round launched in November 2001. Instead, negotiating bilateral and plurilateral free trade agreements (FTAs) increasingly became the central focus of trade policy in the region, more so as the Doha Round faltered and missed its December 2005 deadline for conclusion. The rise of East Asian regionalism further overshadowed APEC. In particular, the ASEAN+3 consisting of ASEAN plus China, Japan and Korea, which was launched informally in December 1997 and institutionalized in 1999, proved an effective platform in dealing with the Asian crisis. Other East Asia groupings have since been established.

Commitment to the Bogor goals and the IAPs continued to be reaffirmed in the AELM declarations in the years after the Asian crisis, except the one issued in Sydney in 2007. Initiatives to improve the IAPs were also undertaken, including: the introduction of peer reviews in 1997; adoption of the Shanghai Accord in 2001 that included measures such as scheduling a mid-term stocktake of overall progress in 2005, strengthening the peer review process, and trade facilitation; and adoption of the Busan Roadmap in 2005 and the Hanoi Action Plan to implement the Busan Roadmap in 2006, which went beyond the liberalization agenda.

The 2005 mid-term stocktake report noted that "APEC has made momentous strides towards free and open trade and investment." It also concluded that the

APEC AT 20: RETROSPECT AND PROSPECT (continued)

Bogor goals continued to be as relevant as in 1994. But it also recognized the significantly changed trade and business environment, which called for APEC to adapt its focus accordingly. In particular, the report argued that the focus should be expanded beyond border issues to include business facilitation and behind-the-border issues such as structural and regulatory reform if the Bogor goals are to be met. But the report did not explicitly state if the Bogor goals are expected to be met, particularly the 2010 deadline.

The explicit link between meeting the Bogor goals and structural and regulatory reform was first made in the 1999 Leaders Declaration, which also endorsed a set of principles to enhance competition and regulatory reform. Subsequent declarations also highlighted the importance of structural reform, and commitment to accelerating structural reform in APEC. The Leaders' Agenda to Implement Structural Reform (LAISR) was then adopted in 2004, which identified five priority areas: regulatory reform, competition policy, public sector management, corporate governance and strengthening economic and legal infrastructure. In 2005, the APEC Work Plan on LAISR towards 2010 (LAISR 2010) was adopted, which set out a roadmap to address structural reform issues across APEC over the next five years consistent with the LAISR declaration. In August 2008, Australia hosted the first Structural Reform Ministerial Meeting. The meeting adopted a "Good Practice Guide on Regulatory Reform", which member economies could use to conduct voluntary assessments of their regulations.

As noted earlier, there was no explicit mention of the Bogor goals in the 2007 Leaders Declaration issued in Sydney, which focused exclusively on climate change, energy security and clean development. Any reference to open trade and investment was made in that context. Instead, the leaders issued a statement on the Doha Development Round, and adopted a report on strengthening regional economic integration that set out a three-year programme on trade, investment and economic reform. APEC's commitment to the Bogor goals was reaffirmed in the report, but it also identified a Free Trade Area of the Asia Pacific (FTAAP) as a possible long term prospect for APEC. The report also entailed "a commitment to new emphasis on structural reform and to addressing 'behind the border' impediments to trade, economic growth and productivity improvement".

There were early proposals to create a FTAAP even while APEC was still in its inception. But to most people, it was an idea whose time had not yet come. It was only in 2004 that the FTAAP was first mentioned in a Leaders Declaration. In particular, the leaders acknowledged two proposals presented to them by the APEC Business Advisory Council (ABAC), one of which was a study of the feasibility and potential scope and features of a FTAAP. But the leaders expressed agreement with ABAC only on the critical importance of trade facilitation and sought its views on issues related to trade facilitation and the increasing number of regional trading arrangements and free trade agreements (RTAs/FTAs) among the member economies. RTAs/FTAs are officially viewed as contributing to the achievement of the Bogor goals and advancing the WTO process, albeit subject to certain conditions. In fact, APEC meetings have served as venues for such discussions and negotiations. Thus, the focus in APEC has been on identifying best practices to promote greater coherence and "high quality" RTAs/FTAs in the region.

Finally, in 2006 the leaders gave instructions "to undertake further studies on ways and means to promote regional economic integration, including a Free Trade Area of the Asia-Pacific as a long-term prospect". This was the REI report adopted at the 2007 meeting. The recent focus on a FTAAP is supposedly not meant to supplant the Bogor goals. Rather, it is seen as a means to achieve the Bogor goals, and as a natural extension of the proliferation of RTAs/FTAs that could eliminate the "spaghetti bowl". Scollay (2004), who drafted the ABAC study, argued that the proposal had to be seen in this perspective. But he also noted that this would mean abandoning APEC's voluntary non-binding approach to commitments and non-discriminatory approach to liberalization.

On the other hand, a study conducted by the Pacific Economic Cooperation Council (PECC) and ABAC in 2006 to look at the political feasibility of a proposal to establish a FTAAP identified a number of practical difficulties. These include the multiple bilateral and regional trade agreements currently under consideration by APEC members, including a number of configurations that include only "Asian" economies (PECC 2007).

The faltering of APEC's trade liberalization agenda led to a search for an alternative trade agenda that was broader in scope. In addition, APEC became involved in prevailing non-economic issues facing the region over the years. In particular, traditional and non-traditional human security issues have formed part of the APEC agenda. Statements and programmes on counter-terrorism have become standard in the aftermath of 11 September 2001. Enhancing human security as an objective in APEC also entailed measures to address pandemics such as HIV/AIDS, SARS, avian flu and influenza, as well as emergency preparedness and disaster response. The most recent initiatives relate to the environment, including climate change and energy security, and food security as well corporate social responsibility.

APEC AT 20: RETROSPECT AND PROSPECT (continued)

Prospect

The year 2009 marks the 20th anniversary of the first APEC ministerial meeting in Canberra, while 2010 is the deadline set for the developed member economies of APEC to achieve the Bogor goals of free and open trade and investment adopted in 1994.

Some things are vastly different twenty years hence, both with respect to APEC itself and the environment in which it operates. APEC now consists of twenty-one member economies with an expanded agenda. Consequently, the number of meetings has significantly increased as well. In addition to the annual meetings of heads of government and key ministers, numerous other meetings are conducted by ABAC and a large number of committees, working groups and task forces.

APEC leaders and officials seem pleased with their overall progress as indicated in their various declarations and statements. In particular, in response to the 2005 mid-term stocktake report, the leaders noted that they "are convinced that both our individual and collective efforts towards the Bogor Goals have contributed to rapid and sustained economic growth as well as to significant improvements in the welfare of our people". That APEC has played a key role in promoting trade and investment liberalization, and facilitating dialogue and cooperation within the Asia-Pacific region not just on trade related issues cannot be disputed. The question is, how critical has it really been? More importantly, will it play a critical role in the region in the years ahead?

Recent public sentiment seems to indicate otherwise. PECC's annual survey of opinion leaders in the region in 2007 indicate that only 48 per cent of those surveyed agreed with the statement that "APEC is as important today as it was in 1989" (PECC 2007). The survey also showed that "lack of commitment from key member economies", "lack of relevance to issues facing ordinary citizens", and "lack of focus on relevant issues" were deemed as among the most important issues facing APEC as an institution, while the Doha Round and FTAAP were identified as the top policy priorities that APEC should focus on.

APEC has been criticized for spending too much time talking and not enough time doing; being strong on goals but weak on achievements; and easily diverted by other issues at the expense of its core agenda. On the other hand, it has also been argued that: the regular meetings among leaders, officials and stakeholders have helped to develop important networks and a habit and mindset of cooperation; it is difficult to precisely measure the contribution and achievements of APEC because it is not a rules-based or negotiating forum; it has promoted best practices and international standards; and its flexibility in identifying and dealing with key issues is one of the strengths of the APEC process. In particular, the AELM lends itself very well to an agenda that goes beyond trade simply because of its composition.

Although it has been argued that significant progress has been achieved in key areas of liberalization and facilitation, the consensus is that the Bogor goals are not likely to be met. It has also been argued that "failure to meet the Bogor goals does not in itself invalidate the importance of APEC" (PECC 2007, p. 6). The argument has been made that the Bogor goals were unrealistic to begin with, given the non-binding, voluntary nature of APEC agreements. But it will further undermine APEC's credibility, unless it is able to sufficiently demonstrate its success in some other tangible way. After all, the Bogor goals constitute its main agenda, and failure to achieve it brings into question APEC's capacity and will to truly advance trade and investment liberalization in the region.

The role and relevance of APEC has been the subject of various studies and discussions in recent years, especially since the institutional landscape in the region has also changed significantly. In addition to ASEAN and APEC, countries in Southeast Asia are also now involved in ASEAN+3, East Asia Summit (EAS), Asia-Europe Meeting (ASEM), and Asia Cooperation Dialogue (ACD), among other regional initiatives. Various options and strategies to reshape and transform APEC have also been put forward, ranging from simple administrative changes to a complete overhaul. Some changes are already being made, particularly in terms of strengthening the secretariat. Whatever further changes APEC decides to make, the bottom line is that after twenty years, the only way for APEC to regain/sustain public support is to demonstrate truly tangible benefits that are unique to APEC. Thus, part of the challenge for APEC in 2009–2010 will be "to find a new way of articulating the organization's raison d'etre and new approaches for promoting more open trade and investment in the region" (PECC 2007, p. 6).

Two of the main economic issues that will be faced by the Asia-Pacific region in 2009, together with the rest of the world, are the impending global economic slowdown as a result of the credit crunch in the aftermath of the U.S. financial crisis, which had strong spillover effects on global financial markets; and failure to conclude the WTO's Doha Development Round. How APEC responds to these issues will also have a bearing on its ability to regain momentum and confidence. But that does not mean a dramatic or large-scale response is necessarily called for. Ravenhill (2007) and Nesadurai (2007), for instance, argue that APEC should focus on "low-key" deliverables, including deepening its work on business facilitation and capacity-building exercises. The key word is "deliverable".

APEC AT 20: RETROSPECT AND PROSPECT (continued)

The 2008 Leaders Declaration has not yet been released when this article was prepared. Given the prevailing global environment, it will most likely address the U.S. financial crisis, which has developed into a truly global financial crisis, and the impending global slowdown. In fact, a statement in the 1997 Leaders Declaration that noted "the global dimensions of these problems suggest the need for a global response" would be more apt in the 2008 statement. Most likely, there will also be a call for the strengthening of financial markets including regulatory and supervisory frameworks similar to the 1997 statement. But a key lesson from the 1997–1998 experience should not be lost, that is, it is not the time to make any dramatic pronouncement, for instance relating to the FTAAP. Although there should be a strong expression of commitment to what has already been undertaken in terms of trade and investment liberalization, and that there will be no policy reversals. Expression of continued commitment to the conclusion of the Doha Round and the Bogor goals, which are very likely, would also be reassuring. More so if it is accompanied by specific proposed actions.

To prepare for its chairmanship, Singapore hosted the APEC Symposium in October 2008, which was attended by APEC senior officials responsible for trade and finance policies, and private sector representatives. The objective was "to discuss and generate new ideas on what APEC can do to fulfill its mission of facilitating economic growth, cooperation, trade and investment in the Asia-Pacific". The initial, partial agenda presented by Singapore at the Symposium can be described as "low-key" or pragmatic in that there was no attempt to reinvent the wheel. Rather, the emphasis was to ensure continuity by building on the work programme undertaken by earlier host economies, Australia and Peru, while coordinating with the next host economy, Japan.

One of the key areas that Singapore plans to focus on is deepening the work on regional economic integration. In particular, work will be undertaken in three areas: (i) accelerate trade and investment liberalization (at the border); (ii) improve business environment (behind the border); and (iii) enhance connectivity (across the border).

The proposed work programme on trade liberalization will have a strong emphasis on the technical aspect. That is, further analytical work will be done on how to advance the trade agenda, including analytical work on the FTAAP, and on the convergence and divergence of the various RTAs/FTAs and the various options such as docking, merging and enlargement. The focus of regulatory reforms will be on improving the business environment, particularly regulations that directly affect business. Finally, enhancing connectivity will include further work on trade logistics and transport networks.

On the Doha Round, the hope is that APEC will play a similar role the way it did with the Uruguay Round. But the delineation in terms of key players is not as clear cut today; that is, breaking the impasse does not just involve resolving differences between member economies of APEC and the EU. There are other key players today, particularly India and Brazil. Also, APEC was very new during the Uruguay Round, which is why the U.S. "gambit" of announcing "a community of Asia Pacific economies" as APEC vision worked. Now the rest of the world is wiser to what APEC can and cannot do.

Of the thirty-five bilateral and six plurilateral FTAs existing in the Asia-Pacific region in 2008, one plurilateral FTA has been identified as capable of playing a potentially critical role in integrating the region. The Trans-Pacific Strategic Economic Partnership Agreement, also known P4, is a plurilateral free trade agreement between the countries of Brunei, Chile, New Zealand and Singapore. Negotiations were launched at the 2002 AELM in Mexico. The agreement was finally signed in 2005 and came into force in 2006. One of its objectives is to contribute to Asia-Pacific wide regional economic integration, by serving as a model trade agreement for the region that could potentially attract new members. The agreement is open to accession "on terms to be agreed among the parties, by any APEC economy or other state".

The U.S. agreed to join the P4 members in February 2008 in negotiations over investment and trade in financial services, which are not part of P4. In September 2008, the U.S. announced its decision to enter negotiations into joining the P4 Agreement itself. Other APEC member economies have also been reported to express interest in joining the agreement, including Australia, Peru and Vietnam. Whether this move will have a similar impact in terms of prodding the other key players to revive and finally conclude the Doha Round remains to be seen. Whether it will play a key role in reviving APEC also remains to be seen. The difficulty of negotiating an FTA with the U.S., particularly for developing economies cannot be underestimated. Finally, it should be noted that the U.S wanted to negotiate over trade in financial services. In the context of the current global financial crisis, liberalizing trade in financial services is something that developing APEC member economies should handle with extreme caution.

Clearly APEC has to deal with some key issues if it is to become truly relevant in the years ahead. And this is best done in the context of the existing

APEC AT 20: RETROSPECT AND PROSPECT (continued)

regional institutional architecture, and how it should evolve in the next ten years or so. But significant changes cannot happen without a change in the mindset by member economies, including those in Southeast Asia. Ultimately, the impact of APEC in the member economies in Southeast Asia will also depend on their level of commitment to and participation in the APEC process and agenda.

Table 1: APEC Members

1989	1991	1993	1994	1998
Australia	People's Republic of	Mexico	Chile	Peru
Brunei Darussalam	China	Papua New		Russia
Canada	Hong Kong, China	Guinea		Vietnam
Indonesia	Chinese Taipei			
Japan				
Republic of Korea				
Malaysia				
New Zealand				
Philippines				
Singapore				
Thailand				
United States				

SOURCE: APEC website <www.apec.org>.

References

Eminent Persons Group. *A Vision for APEC Towards an Asia Pacific Economic Community*. A report submitted to the APEC Ministers, October 1993.

Janow, E.M. *APEC: An Assessment*. Discussion Paper no. 3, APEC Study Centre, Columbia University, 2007.

Nesadurai, H. "APEC and East Asia: The Challenge of Remaining Relevant". In *APEC and the Search for Relevance: 2007 and Beyond*, edited by L. Elliott, J. Ravenhill, H. Nesadurai and N. Bisley. Canberra: Australian National University, 2007.

Pacific Economic Cooperation Council. *State of the Region 2007–2008*. PECC International Secretariat, Singapore, 2007.

Ravenhill, J. "From Poster Child to Orphan: The Rise and Demise of APEC". In *APEC and the Search for Relevance: 2007 and Beyond*, edited by L. Elliott, J. Ravenhill, H. Nesadurai and N. Bisley. Canberra: Australian National University, 2007.

Scollay, R. Preliminary assessment of the proposal for a Free Trade Area of the Asia-Pacific (FTAAP). An issues paper prepared for the APEC Business Advisory Council, Singapore, 2004.

FOOD CRISIS IN SOUTHEAST ASIA: WHAT CAUSED? WHAT NEXT?

By Aekapol Chongvilaivan

A ll over the world, rapidly rising food prices have made basic food commodities — rice, maize, wheat, and soybean — unaffordable for the poor. According to the *International Financial Statistics* (IFS), the world food price index has increased 86 per cent since 2000 — 68.6 per cent for Malaysia's palm oil, 77.3 per cent for Thailand's rice, and 50.9 per cent for the Philippines' coconut oil. The United States Department of Agriculture estimated that "some 130 million additional people have joined the ranks of the hungry due to the global food crisis" (World Food Programme 2008) — 80 per cent of whom are the poorest, most vulnerable women and children.

Food Price Inflation in Southeast Asian Countries
Unavoidably, Southeast Asian countries have also been suffering from what the United Nations' World Food Programme (WFP) coined a "silent tsunami" of a global food crisis that propelled millions of the poor into drastic starvation and malnutrition. This food price catastrophe has become a threat of food security in this region.

Figure 1: The Monthly Trends of the World Food and Energy Prices

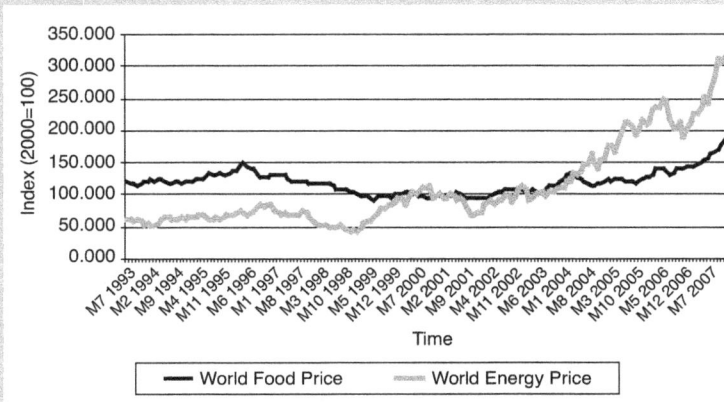

Source: International Financial Statistics (IFS), International Monetary Fund.

FOOD CRISIS IN SOUTHEAST ASIA: WHAT CAUSED? WHAT NEXT? (continued)

A Rice Crisis in the Philippines: The Philippines, the world's largest rice importer, was severely affected by nearly tripled prices of rice — from US$400 a ton in January to more than US$1,000 in April 2008. The rice price turmoil spurred rice stampedes even if the government has painstakingly attempted to secure alternative rice sources to offset the effects of the rice export restrictions imposed by major rice-exporting countries, including India, Indonesia and Vietnam.

Skyrocketing Food Price Inflation in Indonesia: The food crisis entailed nearly double-digit food price inflation in the mid of 2008. This had largely affected the livelihoods of farmers and consumers and had provoked protests in many parts of Indonesia.

Rice Hoarding in Vietnam: Even though Vietnam is one of the world's largest rice-exporting countries, doubled rice prices have caused economy-wide chaos — shoppers rushed to buy up and store rice. As a result, the government banned the aggressive speculation, hoarding and pre-emptive buying and imposed export restrictions to curb its domestic rice price inflation.

Food Shortages in Burma: Burma has undergone a long-lasting economic slump since the nation-wide strife in September 2007. Millions of people live with daily income less than US$2 a day, of which 75 per cent goes toward daily nourishment, and hence are miserably affected by skyrocketing food prices.

Malnourishment in Cambodia: The food crisis has drastically undermined food security in Cambodia. It has been reported that WFP inevitably ceased rice supplies for more than 400,000 students in March 2008 as the rice procurement failed due mainly to exponentially soaring rice prices and unprecedentedly serious rice shortages.

Political Instability in Malaysia: The food price spikes are a political issue in Malaysia which deteriorated its political stability. Opposition parties doubted the ruling party's performance of controlling domestic food prices and ensuring food security during the general election in March 2008.

However, the worldwide surge in grain prices has provided rice farmers in rice-exporting countries economic opportunities. Rice farming in Thailand, for instance, has become highly lucrative as rice prices are more than doubled — with the price of Thai Grade B rice in April 2008 tripled from the level last year.

Global Energy Crisis, Biofuels Craze and Food Shortages
Economists postulate a number of fundamental factors that account for the recent upsurge in food prices — global warming and climate change that caused long-lasting droughts in sub-Saharan Africa, Australia, the Philippines and other parts of the world; trade liberalization and agricultural subsidies in the U.S. and the EU that wiped out farm land in Mexico and the Philippines; and fast growing demand for food consumption by large developing countries, especially China and India, which entails sharp declines in global grain stocks; and the global energy price crisis (Trostle 2008).

Among these factors, the global energy crisis — the world energy prices have been tripled since 2000 — has been unanimously and consistently acknowledged as the most significant culprit of the food price turmoil (Cocoran 2008 and Kingsbury 2007 among others). In fact, the relationship between the energy price shocks and the skyrocketing food prices is not straightforward and requires thorough understandings. There are a number of mechanisms through which the global energy crisis explains rapidly soaring food prices.

Firstly, energy costs have a major role to play in explaining the food price hikes since the advancement of agricultural technology and industrialization have made modern food production highly reliant on petroleum-based intermediate inputs and services — fertilizers, equipment and transportation. Therefore, the energy price shocks directly trigger sweeping surges in costs of food production.

Secondly, spiraling food markets induced investors and speculators into commodity futures markets serving as a hedge against commodity price risk. This argument seems highly probable given that the commodity trading systems in Southeast Asian countries are integrated and are dominated by industrial farms, i.e. Thai multinational Charoen Pokphand (CP) Group.

Last and most importantly, the global energy crisis has brought about the international biofuels stampede which contributed enormously to the global food crisis. Skyrocketing energy prices resulted in energy security concerns, triggering the boom of the biofuel industry. The US$100-a-barrel oil has induced farmers to leave out food and grain production and transform their arable land towards agrofuels production, i.e. palm oil, coconut oil, sugar cane and tapioca. According to the World Bank's recent report, the biofuels craze explains 75 per cent increases in global food prices.

As in developed countries, especially in the United States, the European Union and Canada, developing countries in the Southeast Asian region are pursuing perilous energy security policy of biofuels programmes that seriously

FOOD CRISIS IN SOUTHEAST ASIA: WHAT CAUSED? WHAT NEXT? (continued)

fuels the food price calamity. For instance, the Philippines government recently ratified the Biofuels Act, aiming to promote and subsidize biofuels production. Thailand's government likewise introduced a number of measures to uphold private sector's investment in biofuels production, including pre-determined ethanol and biodiesel prices, loan schemes for gasohol production, encouraging the use of ethanol and biodiesel as fuel alternatives. The prevalence of agrofuels and biofuels industries has tremendously done away with the production of staple grains, ultimately accelerating the soaring food prices.

Food Security Policy Challenges
The United Nations Food and Agricultural Organization (FAO) reported that the food prices exhibited a declining trend following the peak in the mid of 2008 as the global food production has increased. Even though the evidence indicates that the recent food crisis is temporary since the food commodity markets tend to adjust to offset external shocks (Sarris 1990), the global food price turmoil and food shortages have become a threat of food security in Southeast Asian countries. Policy challenges for Southeast Asian leaders are as follows.

A New Approach to Energy Security Policy: The current energy security programme to promote the use and production of biofuels and agrofuels contributed significantly to the food shortages in Southeast Asian countries. The resurgence of energy price crises calls for new energy security policy — one that insulates food commodity markets from energy price shocks — that promotes the development and adoption of renewable, environmentally friendly energy sources, i.e. wind-driven generators, solar panels, wind turbines and biomass.

A New Threat of Food Security: Energy price shocks are unlikely to remain the only major source of food price instability. Corporate monopolization in the global food trading system — such as CP Group for industrial farming in Southeast Asia and Archer Daniels Midland, Bunge and Cargill in the global grain trade — is likely to be a new saga of future food crises. It brings about counterproductive speculations and hoarding that destabilize the food markets and implies that farmers will fail to reap benefits from rising food prices. The solution to this problem is straightforward: the leaders must ensure sound competition in the food trading system. Regrettably, the current progress of regional collaboration on food security seems to fortify the threat. Five Southeast Asian countries, including Thailand, Vietnam, Cambodia, Burma and Laos, attempted to establish a beggar-thy-neighbour rice cartel to dominate the global rice market and hence placed the global food security at risk.

References

Cocoran, Terence. "Who Caused the World Food Crisis". *Financial Post*, 8 April 2008.

Kingsbury, Kathleen. "After the Oil Crisis, A Food Crisis?". *Time*, 16 Novermber 2007.

Sarris, Alexandra H. "Has World Cereal Market Instability Increased?". *Food Policy*, vol. 25, no. 3 (2001): 337–50.

Trostle, Ronald. "Global Agricultural Supply and Demand: Factors Contributing to the Recent Increase in Food Commodity Prices". Economic Research Service, no. WRS-0801. Washington: U.S. Department of Agriculture, 2008.

World Food Programme. "Statement by Josette Sheeran Executive Director UN World Food Programme". Available at <http://documents.wfp.org/stellent/groups/public/documents/newsroom/wfp180042.pdf>, 2008.

INCOME INEQUALITIES IN SOUTHEAST ASIA: POTENTIAL FOR MICROFINANCE

By Aparna Bhagirathy Krishnan

Southeast Asian countries have made significant achievements in reducing poverty, particularly extreme poverty. The region is well on track, and is an early achiever in attaining the first Millennium Development Goal (MDG) target of halving extreme poverty[1] by 2015. However, despite this achievement, inequalities persist and are indeed on the rise in the region. The Gini coefficient[2] in most of the countries in the region is over 30 per cent, implying high levels of inequality between the rich and the poor. The only two countries that saw a decline in the Gini index over the past few years are Thailand and Malaysia, though the inequality coefficient in these countries remains over 30 per cent (ESCAP 2007). Another measure, the share of the poor as measured by the poorest quartile in national consumption, has also been declining over the last

---

- Southeast Asia, as a region, has made tremendous progress in reducing extreme poverty. However, inequalities are on the rise, both intra-region, and intra-country. In the absence of specific measures to address poverty and inequality, the gap is only expected to widen.

- In recent years, there has been a lot of attention on microfinance both as a poverty alleviation tool, and as a commercially viable means of delivering financial services to the poor.

- In Southeast Asia, there exists a variety of experiences with microfinance: in some countries, there is a long history of commercial microfinance institutions (such as Indonesia and the Philippines); while in others, the movement is recent, and emerged more by way of a social activity (such as Cambodia and Vietnam). There is scope for further growth and expansion as there is still a lot of unmet potential in the region.

- Recent developments in the sector and challenges imposed by the global financial crisis this year may accelerate the trend of commercialization of the microfinance sector in the region.

---

[1] Extreme poverty refers to percentage of population living under $1/day.
[2] A comprehensive measure of income inequality, ranging from 0 (absolute equality) to 100 (absolute inequality).

decade in the Philippines, Lao PDR, Cambodia and Malaysia. This means that as these countries grow, the gap between the rich and the poor widens and the poor have a smaller share every year in the national consumption.

There are also differences in achievements between countries within the region. While the average poverty rate of countries in Southeast Asia is about 8 per cent, the poverty rate among the least developed countries of the region is about 34 per cent (Asia-Pacific MDG Study Series 2007). Vicious cycles of inequality when reinforced, could lead to social and/or political instability, and undermine future achievements of goals such as universal education, health, sanitation, etc. (Asia-Pacific MDG Study Series 2007). Poverty reinforces vulnerabilities, and these in turn, lead to other types of disparities — inequalities in access to health facilities, to safe drinking water and sanitation, to formal financial markets, etc.

The global food crisis earlier this year, particularly soaring rice prices has adversely affected the well being of the poor in most developing countries, and could reverse some of the progress made in reducing poverty levels. The United Nations World Food Programme (WFP) characterized the soaring food prices as the "silent tsunami" threatening to push an additional 100 million people worldwide into hunger. Some have pointed to the other side of the argument, which is that rising food prices also mean that they are beneficial for farmers in the long run. The problem however, is that in most developing countries given the majority of small farmers, and given the shortage of investments in agriculture and infrastructure, it is questionable if these farmers would be in a position to take advantage of the short-term price rises.

Poor people when exposed to shocks in the short or long run — of income, consumption, health, or weather — often have limited mechanisms to cope with them. They often use *ex post* mechanisms, such as borrowing and informal social transfers, which are inadequate when shocks are aggregate (such as a flood), or are of a large scale. Yet, they often do not have access to *ex ante* mechanisms, such as insurance, savings, or other financial instruments, which can help to manage risks better because they are excluded from formal financial markets. Recently, there has been a lot of attention on an innovative means of delivering financial services to the poor, through microfinance. Microfinance refers to the provision of a broad range of financial services such as deposits, loans, payment

INCOME INEQUALITIES IN SOUTHEAST ASIA: POTENTIAL FOR MICROFINANCE (continued)

services, money transfers and insurance to poor and low-income households and their microenterprise (ADB 2000).

The Nobel Peace Prize 2006 was awarded to the Grameen Bank of Bangaldesh and its founder, Muhammad Yunus, for "their efforts to create economic and social development from below". The MDGs 2020 Vision recognizes microfinance as a crucial tool for poverty alleviation. Microfinance seeks to remove an important barrier for the growth of small enterprises through providing access to credit, and financial instruments such as insurance in order to enhance the risk taking capacities of the poor, and in turn improve the return on their businesses and incomes.

In addition to serving as a potential means of combating poverty, recent developments in the microfinance sector across the world suggest that it could also be a business tool for providing financial services to the urban and rural poor. At the recent Microcredit Summit in Bali, in July 2008, Planet Finance estimated that in South and East Asia (excluding India and China), there are still more than 140 million poor people to be reached by any sort of financial service. The Microfinance Information Exchange (MIX) data shows that microfinance penetration rates in Southeast Asia are still low. Microfinance programmes in some of the most populous countries, Indonesia and the Philippines, reach only 11 per cent and 6 per cent of their poor respectively. In Bangladesh, home to the Grameen Bank, microfinance programmes have been successful at reaching 35 per cent of their poor.

Southeast Asia represents a region with an interesting range of developments in the microfinance sector. It comprises of countries with a long history of commercially viable formal financial institutions providing microfinance, such as in Indonesia since the 1980s. The best known microfinance institution (MFI), also the largest in the world, is the Bank Rakyat Indonesia's (BRI) Micro Business Division, known as BRI Units (Charitonenko and Fernando 2004). The Philippines has traditionally been dominated by credit cooperatives and non-governmental organizations (NGOs); commercialization is a recent phenomenon, promoted by the government. Some of the larger NGOs have in recent years, successfully converted themselves into microfinance banks. Microfinance is relatively more recent in Laos, Cambodia and Vietnam. In Laos and Cambodia, such initiatives have been primarily led by NGOs, since formal financial markets are anyway not yet developed fully. However, in Cambodia, ACLEDA Bank represents a successful transformation of a NGO into a microfinance bank in the year 2000. Vietnam has seen dramatic expansion of microfinance activity over the last few years, spearheaded almost solely by the Vietnam Bank for Social Policies (VBSP), a State-led initiative. However, VBSP serves a much broader audience than just the poor, and the government heavily subsidizes the programme. This raises concerns about the commercial viability of the programme.

Commercialization of microfinance is gaining currency rapidly in Asia, even amidst several concerns in the sector of such developments causing a mission drift away from serving the poor. However, commercialization still holds the promise of rapidly reaching large proportions of the poor, excluded from any sort of finance. Since 2000, there has been a rapid increase in the number of for-profit commercial MFIs.[3] In a study of the growth of commercial microfinance between 2005–2006, 222 MFIs were identified around the world as regulated and shareholder-owned institutions. The study shows that Asian MFIs serve more than 50 per cent of clients worldwide but account for only 26 per cent of the US$1.5 billion equity investments in the sector across the world (Rhyne and Busch 2006). Even though MFIs in Southeast Asia are not growing as quickly as the institutions in South Asia, the values of microfinance loan portfolios are much larger. Further, of the equity investments in Asia, which is a little over US$400 million, the MFIs in Southeast Asia[4] account for more than 80 per cent of these investments[5] (Rhyne and Busch 2006). Emerging economies of Vietnam, Cambodia and Laos are likely to be the most promising areas in the region for growth of microfinance in the next few years. Overall, the trend of commercialization of MFIs is likely to continue.

As more information becomes available on MFI growth and profitability, it has also started to attract the attention of private investors. The MIX currently lists over 100 specialized microfinance investment funds that invest in MFIs across the world. It is expected that the current financial crisis may affect the microfinance industry in some countries to a certain extent. MFIs solely dependent on commercial bank loans (which remains a primary source of funding for several MFIs) would have to face a liquidity crunch. However, the MFI sector can also use the opportunity to present themselves as promising investment avenues for private investors looking for new ventures.

---

[3] These include commercial banks entering microfinance, NGOs establishing microfinance banks, non-banking financial institutions, and equity investments in microfinance.
[4] The study includes about twenty-two microfinance banks and financial institutions from Indonesia, Cambodia and the Philippines.
[5] Calculated from data contained in the Rhyne and Busch (2006) study.

INCOME INEQUALITIES IN SOUTHEAST ASIA: POTENTIAL FOR MICROFINANCE (continued)

The microfinance sector today is composed of a wide variety of players, ranging from government-sponsored programmes to private equity funds. It is no longer a charitable or social activity; it is now a commercially viable proposition. In order to promote further investment in the microfinance sector, clear and transparent information on operations and financial performance of MFIs are required. In what has now come to be known as the second generation of microfinance, challenges will be in developing regulation and the policy environment to sustain rapid growth of these institutions. Several practitioners are concerned of a potential microfinance bubble that may burst with rapid growth and large amounts of investment flowing too quickly into the sector. At the organizational end, institutions must focus on developing innovative and flexible products in order to reduce some of the rigidities of the existing systems. Continuous innovations on the ground coupled with rigorous evaluations of these programmes will provide much needed evidence on the effectiveness of microfinance as a vehicle for delivering financial products for the poor; and the impact of microfinance on improving the economic and social well-being of its clients, the poor.

References

ADB. *Finance for the Poor: Microfinance Development Strategy*. Asian Development Bank, Manila, 2000.

Asia-Pacific MDG Study Series. *Millennium Development Goals: Progress in Asia and the Pacific 2007*. ESCAP-ADB-UNDP, Bangkok, 2007.

Charitonenko, Anita C., and Nirmal A. Fernando. *Commercialization of Microfinance: Perspectives from South and Southeast Asia*. Asian Development Bank, Manila, 2004.

Rhyne, Elisabeth and Bryan Busch. *The Growth of Commercial Microfinance: 2004-2006*. Council of Microfinance Equity Funds, 2006.

ESCAP. *Statistical Yearbook for Asia and the Pacific*. United Nations, New York, 2007.

Microfinance Information Exchange (MIX). <www.themix.org> and <www.mixmarket.org>.

THE ASEAN-10

Lee Poh Onn • Jayant Menon • Reza Siregar •
Kyophilavong Phouphet • Kian-Teng Kwek •
Mya Than • Aladdin D. Rillo • Manu Bhaskaran •
Sakulrat Montreevat • Nick J. Freeman

Brunei Darussalam

2009 and 2010 will be challenging for the Bruneian economy in terms of its growth prospects. This is because of a major downturn in economies like the United States, Japan and the European Union. The first two are major trading partners of Brunei Darussalam.

The financial crisis which erupted with the U.S. subprime mortgage in late 2007 has deepened into a global financial crisis since September 2008. The impacts of this crisis are also now increasingly felt by emerging economies around the world and also in ASEAN. This financial shock coupled with the still high commodity and energy prices is expected to push the world economy into a recession in 2009.

BRUNEI DARUSSALAM

- The economic outlook is challenging for Brunei Darussalam with growth expected to be about 1 and 2 per cent for 2009 to 2010 respectively, because of the global financial crisis and the slowdown in the U.S., Japanese, EU and ASEAN economies.

- Oil prices have fallen in late 2008 because of the global downturn and this is also expected to impact on Brunei Darussalam's growth prospects in 2009.

- Economic diversification is continuing with the development of ecotourism, the halal and food industry, the Sungai Liang Industrial Park, and the development of Pulau Muara Besar. This would help to buffer the country's slowdown to a certain extent.

Latest Available Demographic and Economic Data

First some of the latest available basic demographic and economic data prior to the forecast period of 2009 and 2010. Brunei had a recorded population of about 393,000 as at mid-2008. The annual rate of population growth rate decreased from 3.5 per cent in 2006 to 1.8 per cent in 2007.[1] In the same period, the labour force participation rate decreased from 71.7 per cent in 2006 to 71.2 per cent in 2007. Unemployment stood at 3.4 per cent in 2007 and is expected to stay more or less the same in 2008.[2] Real GDP will probably be in the negative zone in 2008 of about –0.5 per cent. This is in contrast to 5.1 per cent growth in 2006 and 0.6 per cent in 2007.[3]

The production of oil (barrels/day) in Brunei has decreased from 219,258 barrels in 2006 to 193,832 barrels in 2007.[4] The fall was attributed to a strategic curtailing in order to protect some wells, as well as some other existing and new wells not producing as anticipated. Production is again expected to hover around the 200,000 mark in 2008 and in subsequent years. Gas production for which data is available for 2005 to 2006 indicates an increase of 4.6 per cent.[5] Inflation will still be under control during the forecast period, about 1 per cent and 1.2 in 2009 and 2010 respectively.[6]

Growth Forecast for 2009 and 2010

Based on the IMF, *World Economic Outlook Database* in October 2008[7] and the author's own estimates, the growth forecast in Brunei Darussalam will be at 1 and 2 per cent for 2009 and 2010 respectively. Growth will revert to the positive from 2009 onwards because of the continuing development of Brunei's ecotourism industry, progress in the methanol plant project, and the continuing development of Sungai Liang Industrial Park (SPark) project, among others.

Of course, high petroleum prices prevailing throughout most of 2008 and possibly picking up in the latter part of 2009 are expected to shore up Brunei's growth in the next few years. Remembering that the oil and gas sector made up 57.2 per cent of GDP in 2007,[8] with this trend expected to continue during the forecast period.

The higher oil and gas prices in the last quarter of 2007 which hit US$96 per barrel would maintain the revenue base and fiscal surplus balance as well as Brunei's overall trade balance surplus for 2008 and the years thereafter. Oil hit a high of US$147.27 on 11 July 2008, although it later dropped to about US$50 per barrel in November 2008. Analysts expect prices to pick up once again when the current economic downturn in the world's major economies bottom out and regain their momentum upwards in the latter part of 2009. Global growth is expected to moderate from 3.9 per cent in 2008 to 3 per cent in 2009.[9]

The current downturn in the U.S. is a major reason for the massive dip in oil prices. This serves as a double whammy for Brunei during the forecast period of growth. First, it is now evident that the global financial crisis and the downturn in the U.S. economy have affected economies around the world. Reportedly, the U.S. may only recover in late 2009. Lower oil prices also means lower revenues for Brunei.

Many of Brunei's other trading partners have also reported slowdowns in their economies in 2008 which is expected to continue in the first three quarters of 2009.[10] Brunei's major export markets in 2007[11] include Australia (13.7 per cent), Indonesia (24.2 per cent), Japan (33.5 per cent), the Republic of Korea (12.1 per cent) and the USA (5 per cent), all of which are reportedly heading towards decelerations in their economic growth rates in 2008 and 2009. Notably, Indonesia and Japan account for about 60 per cent of Brunei's export market.

Exports in 2007 were dominated by oil and gas which accounted for 96.2 per cent of Brunei's total exports.[12] To the extent that the growth prospects of these countries have been affected by the current downturn, so will the Brunei's economy be influenced to move in tandem with developments in these economies. In terms of gas, Japan is the largest importer (about 92 per cent of Brunei's total output).

Policy-makers in Brunei realise that the economy is currently too dependent on oil and gas. It has been reported that supplies of oil in the country are expected to run out in about twenty years' time. As such, future growth prospects must look beyond oil and gas into the other relatively undeveloped sectors in the Bruneian economy that could prove promising to the country in the medium- to long-term prospects of economic growth.

Developments Influencing the Growth Forecast Lie in Economic Diversification

What are the developments that will bode well for Brunei during the forecast period?

Brunei's literacy rates are among the highest in ASEAN with an adult literacy rate of 96.5 per cent for males and 93.1 per cent for females. Brunei is ranked 30th best in terms of the Human Development Index.[13]

Diversification is beginning to show its fruit. From the latest figures available, the non-oil and gas sector has helped to boost year-on-year GDP with growth rates in 2007 of about 9.5 per cent. Government services recorded the highest growth rate (15.7 per cent increase), followed by the private sector of about 5.9 per cent.[14]

Brunei has another draw card for diversification in that it can also build on its ecotourism industry.

Heart of Borneo Project

The Heart of Borneo (HoB) Declaration which was signed on 12 February 2007 by the Governments of Brunei Darussalam, Indonesia and Malaysia has gained further traction. This declaration involves the conservation and sustainable management of one of the most important areas of biological diversity, covering approximately 220,000 km² of equatorial rainforests.

In October 2008, Brunei Shell Petroleum and the Hong Kong and Shanghai Bank has donated about US$333,000 each to conserve forests in Brunei.[15] This would go towards the establishment of the Heart of Borneo Brunei Center that will implement the Heart of Borneo initiative.

The Standard Chartered Bank also donated US$500,000 to the Heart of Borneo Project. The first two projects that will benefit from this donation are the rehabilitation of Borneo's peatland forest, and the biodiversity survey of the Sungai Ingei protection forest to aid an understanding of the resources available, the discovery of new species and new ways to preserve biodiversity.[16] Standard Chartered Bank is joined by the British High Commission in the project.

Pulau Muara Besar Deepwater Container Port

The development of Pulau Muara Besar as a deepwater container port, export processing zone, and manufacturing hub is another plus factor for Brunei. In October 2008, the Memorandum of Understanding (MoU) was signed with port operator International Container Terminal Services Inc (ICTSI) from the Philippines, and the Master Planner agreement with the Surbana consortium from Singapore.[17]

The Pulau Muara Besar master plan includes developing an export processing zone for halal food, and a manufacturing complex for major industries including the possible establishment of an aluminium smelter to complement the port's operations. Tenders for major infrastructural projects in the port will be called in 2010.

The development of this container port will provide a boost in business opportunities for investors and contractors, local as well as foreign, and this would represent a new sector of potential growth, as well as aiding in Brunei's quest for diversification. In the forecast period, the development of this port and its related activities are expected to underpin growth in Brunei's construction sector.[18]

Sungai Liang Industrial Park

A huge potential exists for extending the oil and gas value chain in Brunei. At the Sungai Liang Industrial Park (SPark), Brunei is planning a world class petrochemical hub.[19] The first investor in SPark is the Brunei Methanol Company, formed by a partnership between Brunei's National Oil Company, Petroleum Brunei, and two leading Japanese companies, the Mitsubishi Gas Chemical and Itochu Corporation. When completed at the end of 2009, the plant will produce 850,000 tons of methanol per year mostly for export. Commercial production is expected to begin in early 2010.

The Brunei Economic Development Board (BEDB) is in discussions with global investors for a US$1 billion ammonia/urea plant as well as for various methanol spin-off industries, for example, in the manufacture of acetic acid. If the urea project gets lifted off the ground, employment prospects would be expected to improve substantially.

Halal Products

The government is also expected to set up a Halal Products Academy soon to guide and steer the development of what constitutes halal food.[20] This is in line with Brunei's aim to be globally recognized for its quality Islamic food products. Brunei intends to capture part of the international market in halal goods that is worth around US$500 billion dollars.

New Gas Discovery

In November, Total SA announced that it has made a significant gas and condensate discovery off the coast of Brunei.[21] Production from this area is expected to begin by the end of 2008 which would bode well for the Brunei's growth in the forecast period of 2009 and 2010.

NOTES

1. *Key Economic Indicators for Asia and the Pacific 2008*. Philippines: Asian Development Bank, August 2008.
2. Ibid.
3. "Country Report, Brunei". United Kingdom: The Economist Intelligence Unit, September 2008, p. 5.
4. *Brunei Economic Bulletin: Brunei Darussalam Economic Review Outlook and Recent Economic Developments*. Department of Economic Planning and Development, Prime Minister's Office, vol. 5, 2007 Special Edition, May 2008.
5. *Brunei Darussalam: Statistical Appendix*. Washington, D.C.: International Monetary Fund, May 2008.
6. International Monetary Fund (IMF). *World Economic Outlook Database: October 2008 Edition*. < http://www.imf.org > (accessed 21 October 2008).
7. International Monetary Fund (IMF). *World Economic Outlook Database: October 2008 Edition*. < http://www.imf.org > (accessed 21 October 2008).
8. "Country Report, Brunei". United Kingdom: The Economist Intelligence Unit, September 2008, p. 5.
9. *World Economic Outlook October 2008: Financial Stress, Downturns, and Recoveries*. Washington, D.C.: International Monetary Fund, 2008.
10. Ibid.
11. *Brunei Economic Bulletin*, op. cit.
12. Ibid.
13. *Key Economic Indicators for Asia and the Pacific 2008*, op. cit.
14. *Brunei Economic Bulletin*, op. cit.

15. "Shell, HSBC put $665,000 towards Borneo Rainforest Conservation Project", Mongabay.Com, 28 October 2008 < http://news.mongabay.com/2008/1026-borneo.html >.
16. "SCB Donates $700,000 to HoB Project", BruDirect.Com, 27 October 2008 < http://www.brudirect.com/DailyInfo/News/Archive/Oct08/271008/nite02.htm >.
17. "Big Leap towards Realization of PMB", BruDirect.Com, 29 October 2008 < http://www.brudirect.com/DailyInfo/News/Archive/Oct08/291008/nite01.htm >.
18. As an indication, the construction sector is showing very good signs and grew by 10.7 per cent in 2007. See *Brunei Economic Bulletin*, op. cit.
19. The Brunei Forum, co-organised by the Brunei Economic Development Board and the Institute of Southeast Asian Studies, 19–20 February 2008.
20. Halal Academy to Boost Ulama-Industry Ties, *Brunei Times*, 17 August 2008 < http://www.bt.com.bn/en/local_business/2008/08/17/halal_academy_to_boost_ulama_industry_ties >.
21. "Total makes Gas Discovery off the Coast of Brunei", CNNMoney.Com, 3 November 2008 < http://money.cnn.com/news/newsfeeds/articles/apwire/01fe42143be9587794746ad976f009c9.htm >.

Cambodia

GDP growth of 10.1 per cent in 2007 marked the fourth year of double-digit growth in Cambodia, and marked the end of a decade of sustained and robust economic growth that saw a doubling of per capita GDP to $589. This is probably the last year of double-digit growth for some time to come, however, with GDP projected to slow to around 6.5 to 7 per cent in 2008. A turnaround is emerging, with the most spectacular decade of economic growth performance in Cambodia's history coming to a halt. Although growth is likely to moderate, it will continue to be relatively robust, and also more sustainable.

Growth in 2007 was underpinned by the construction, tourism and garment sectors. Nevertheless, there was a significant slowdown in garment exports and a pullback in the expansion of agriculture, both accounting for the moderation in overall growth. Although clothing exports had increased by about 20 per cent in 2006, this growth slowed to an estimated 7 per cent in dollar terms, reflecting increasing competition in the U.S. and EU markets. In agriculture, rice production rose by about 5 per cent to 6 million tons, of which 2 million tons were exported (a ban took effect in 2008). But weaker growth in fisheries and forestry brought overall agriculture growth down to an estimated 4.5 per cent, little changed from that in 2006. The continuing boom in residential and commercial building in Phnom Penh and Siem Reap was a fillip to construction activity.

Growth is expected to slow significantly in 2009 and 2010. The extent of the slowdown will depend mostly on world demand conditions. The latest forecasts for growth in 2009 from the IMF in November 2008 points to a sharp fall to 4.75 per cent, to 6.4 per cent (EIU), to 7 per cent (ADB). The forecasts from ADB and EIU were made prior to the further down-grading of world economic growth by the IMF in November 2008. It is quite plausible that these forecasts may also be brought down in line with the revised IMF view of world economic prospects. The same also applies to official government forecasts, where about 7 per cent growth continues to be expected. Even under the more rosy IMF outlook for world growth, the EIU expects that Cambodia's growth for 2010 will be 6 per cent but this is likely to be revised downwards soon.

Most forecasts point to a slowing in the speed of growth of garment exports in 2008–2009 as a major factor in the slowing of overall growth. The planned lifting of restrictions on Chinese garment exports to the U.S. and the EU at the end of 2008 is likely to significantly affect Cambodia's garment exports. This increase in competition comes on top of a slowing world economy, and therefore a reduction in demand from major markets.

CAMBODIA

- After a decade of spectacular growth, the economy is slowing in response to a global slowdown.

- Despite this, growth is likely to continue to be robust in 2009 and 2010, albeit at a slower but more sustainable pace.

- Dollarization has limited the capacity of monetary authorities to mop up excess liquidity associated with the asset price boom, and therefore has handicapped the implementation of anti-inflationary policies

- Rampant corruption remains a major problem in Cambodia requiring urgent attention.

Cambodia: Selected Economic Indicators, 2007–2010f

	2007	2008E	2009F	2010F
GDP growth (% change)				
ADB	9.6	7.5	7.0	n.a.
IMF	10.2	6.5	4.8	n.a.
EIU	10.1	7.0	6.4	6
– Industry sector growth (% change) (EIU)	15	8	7	7
– Services sector growth (% change) EIU)	10.2	9.4	7.7	7
– Agriculture sector growth (% change) (EIU)	5	2	3.5	3
Exports (US$ million) (EIU)	4,089	4,616	4,997	5345
Imports (US$ million) (EIU)	5,424	6,424	7,017	7454
Trade balance (US$ million) (EIU)	–1,335	–1,809	–2,019	–2109
Current account balance (% of GDP) (EIU)	0.8	–2.5	–1.8	–2
Inflation/CPI average (% change) (ADB)	4.2	5.5	5.0	na
Inflation/CPI average (% change) (EIU)	10.8	17.0	12.6	12.7
M2 money supply growth (% change) (EIU)	61.8	25	24.3	15.9
Fiscal balance (as % of GDP) (EIU)	–1.8	-2	-2	-2
Total debt outstanding (US$ million) (EIU)	3,890	4,317	4,366	4520
Debt service ratio (as % of exports) (EIU)	0.111	0.111	0.110	0.11
Foreign exchange reserves (US$ million) (EIU)	2,143	2,375	2,089	2240
Exchange rate at year-end (CR:US$1) (EIU)	3,580	3,957	4,170	4396

Sources:
ADB. *Asian Development Outlook 2008*. Manila: ADB, 2008.
EIU. *Cambodia Country Report*. EIU, October 2008.
IMF. "Cambodia: 2007 Article IV Consultation — Staff Report; Staff Supplement; and Public Information Notice on the Executive Board Discussion". IMF, Washington, D.C., 2007.
————. "Statement by an IMF Staff Mission to Cambodia". Press Release no. 08/137, IMF, Washington, D.C., July 2008.

Services will continue to thrive, supporting continued growth, with continued increases in finance and trading and, to a lesser extent, tourism, which has already been showing signs of moderating — there has been a sharp drop in tourist arrivals from Korea, the main source country. Construction activity and FDI are also expected to slow, in line with tightening global liquidity conditions.

There was a further narrowing of the fiscal deficit to 1.8 per cent of GDP in 2007. This outcome was a result of higher tax revenues, through improvements in tax administration and collections, and lower capital spending. Forecasts from the EIU see the deficit remaining relatively stable, with only a slight increase to 2.0 per cent in both 2009 and 2010. This would be quite a remarkable achievement on the fiscal front if these forecasts are realized. The overall deficit continues to be financed by concessional loans and grants.

Money supply increased sharply in 2007, with broad money rising by more than 60 per cent. The year on year increase until July 2008 was still a high 37 per cent. In a dollarized economy, inflows of capital in the form of dollars automatically increase the money supply, and the capacity of monetary authorities to do anything about it is limited (more on this below). In July 2008, the National Bank of Cambodia (NBC) doubled the reserve requirement for commercial banks from 8 per cent to 16 per cent, in a vain attempt to limit growth in credit. Again, because of dollarization, capital inflows need not pass through the banking system, rendering this instrument relatively ineffective.

Last year, most forecasters were predicting that inflation was on a downward trend in Cambodia, and that it would soon fall to quite low levels. These forecasts hinged crucially on the assumption that the world price of oil and rice would remain stable. The prices of both these commodities increased sharply, and remain volatile, despite appearing to have already peaked recently. Inflation started rising in 2007, increasing from an average of 4.7 per cent in 2006 to 5.9 per cent. This reflects the initial increases in both food and oil prices. Inflation has increased sharply since then, to an estimated 21.1 per cent in 2008.

According to the latest available figures, consumer prices rose by 22.3 per cent year on year in July 2008, with food prices up by 36.8 per cent. Rice prices rose owing to domestic supply shortages, and prices of other food items also rose, especially meat (pork and chicken). This was a reflection of rising world prices, as well as in response to rising domestic consumption and a ban on meat imports from Vietnam to prevent the spread of animal diseases. Apart from higher global fuel prices, the weakening of the U.S. dollar, which is widely used as money in Cambodia, added to inflation pressure. Consumer price inflation is forecast to fall to an average rate of 12.4 per cent in 2009, with oil prices falling and demand softening as economic growth slows. This trend is likely to continue into 2010, when inflation is expected to fall further to 8.9 per cent.

Dollarization: Help or Hindrance during Crisis?

Cambodia today is still as dollarized, if not more so, than it was ten years ago. The U.S. dollar still serves all the three functions of money: it is widely used as a medium of exchange, store of wealth and unit of account. The IMF estimates the share of dollars in currency in circulation to be about 90 per cent, while the NBC estimates the share of foreign currency deposits in broad money (M2) to have risen to its highest level ever of 75 per cent in 2006. Currently, about 97 per cent of banking deposits are in U.S. dollars.

Dollarization has costs and benefits. These general pros and cons are discussed in Menon (2008*a*, *b*). But is dollarization a good thing or a bad thing during periods of economic instability, and global financial crisis, like the one we are witnessing now? The answer depends in large part on the nature of the challenges faced by the country, especially in terms of the required macroeconomic policy response. On the positive side, the fact that the U.S. dollar is the de facto currency almost rules out any chance of an exchange rate crisis. It may also add further credibility to the macroeconomy by implying stable monetary conditions.

But the asset price boom, especially the land price bubble, has seen a rapid increase in foreign inflows of funds. There are concerns relating to this excess liquidity fuelling inflation, and the inability of the National Bank of Cambodia to mop this up, because of the lack of monetary instruments as a result of dollarization. In particular, the lack of riel-denominated interesting bearing assets limits the ability of the NBC to conduct open market operations. Other monetary instruments, such as changes to the reserve requirement, are likely to be blunt instruments of monetary policy because the dollarization allows capital inflows to become part of the money stock while bypassing the financial system.

In short, dollarization has imposed a constraint during the recent capital surge in Cambodia, preventing monetary authorities from mopping up excess liquidity that spurred inflation in a volatile environment of rising food and oil prices.

Dealing with Corruption

It is an open secret that corruption is more rampant in Cambodia than in many other countries. According to the most recent Corruption Perceptions Index published by Transparency International, Cambodia scored only 1.8 in an index that runs from a score of zero (very corrupt) to ten (very clean). Based on this index, Cambodia was ranked the 14th most corrupt country in the world. What is more disturbing is that corruption appears to be getting worse in Cambodia. This index has fallen from 2.0 in 2007 to 1.8, bringing down its position from 162 to 166 out of 180 countries. There have also been public demonstrations of apparent corrupt practices. In 2006, the World Bank suspended funding for three ongoing infrastructure and water sanitation schemes, worth more than $64 million, after reporting apparent irregularities in seven projects.

There is no doubt that the costs of rampant corruption are very high. Not only does corruption negatively affect economic growth, investment activity, international trade and price stability, it can also bias government expenditure patters. The poor also tend to bear a disproportionately high share of the costs of corruption. With the recent discovery of offshore oil and gas resources in Cambodian territorial waters, there is a greater urgency to ensure that public governance is improved. Large scale resource revenues have been shown to accentuate weaknesses in governance and are closely correlated with increases in corruption and instances of internal conflict. In light of this, what can be done to address, if not reduce, corruption in Cambodia?

Soon after being re-elected this year, Prime Minister Hun Sen declared that his government was determined to improve the state of law and order and to fight corruption. The opposition party has expressed little confidence in the government's ability to do so, however. And there appears to be good reasons to doubt the government's commitment to tackling graft. For instance, it failed to adhere to pledges to pass an anti-corruption law during the previous parliamentary term, despite pressure from foreign donors. On the positive side, a number of important new laws and related regulations were introduced in 2006, which should assist in the fight against corruption. These include a Law on Anti-Money Laundering and Combating Terrorist Financing, Law on Publishing (Issuance) and Trading Non-government Securities, Law on Concessions, Law on Customs and Law on Bankruptcy.

Although the passing of these laws are significant achievement, and that of the impending anti-corruption legislation will be important, it is only likely to succeed in dealing with corruption if fair implementation is assured. This will require improvements in a host of public institutions. As a USAID report lamented, "Large-scale corruption requires broad and diverse institutional support. The Royal Government of Cambodia has developed a full array of outside institutions — captive firms, controlled media, party-affiliated NGOs and unions — as well as the police, military, ministries, judiciary and parliament to support a corrupt system. Until these institutions are reformed, and these affiliations opened up, corruption will continue to constrain Cambodia's development."

REFERENCES

Asian Development Bank. *Asian Development Outlook 2008*. Manila: ADB, 2008.
EIU. *Cambodia Country Report*. EIU, October 2008.
IMF. "Cambodia: 2007 Article IV Consultation — Staff Report; Staff Supplement; and Public Information Notice on the Executive Board Discussion". IMF, Washington, D.C., 2007.
———. "Statement by an IMF Staff Mission to Cambodia". Press Release no. 08/137, IMF, Washington, D.C., July 2008.
———. "Statement at the Conclusion of the 2008 Article IV Discussions with Cambodia". Press Release no. 08/277, 7 November 2008.
Menon, Jayant. "Cambodia's Persistent Dollarization: Causes and Policy Options". *ASEAN Economic Bulletin*, vol. 25, no. 2 (2008a): 228–37.
———. "Dealing with Dollarization: What Options for the Transitional Economies of Southeast Asia?". *Journal of the Asia-Pacific Economy*, vol. 13, no. 2 (2008b): 131–46.
USAID. *Cambodia Corruption Assessment*. USAID and Casal Associates, 2004.
World Bank. *Cambodia: Country Assistance Strategy of the World Bank Group, 2005–2008*. Phnom Penh: World Bank Cambodia Country Office, 2005.
———. *Halving Poverty by 2015: Cambodia Poverty Assessment*. Phnom Penh: World Bank Cambodia Country Office, 2006.

INDONESIA

Forecasting key macroeconomic indicators have become more and more difficult under the current global market conditions. From January to October 2008, the Jakarta Composite Index (JCI) has declined by close to 60 per cent, with much of the drop took place between September to October 2008. Massive sell-offs led to the suspension of trading activities of the afternoon session at the JCI on Wednesday, 8 October 2008, and the market was only reopened on Monday, 13 October 2008. That was the first suspension in eight years and was the worst weekly decline of the index in twenty-five years. Between October 2007 to August 2008 alone, the total capitalization of the Indonesia stock exchange has fallen by as much as 4 per cent of GDP.

The sell-offs in the capital market led to depreciation pressure on the local currency, Rupiah, and forced the monetary authority to intervene actively in the foreign exchange market. However, despite the frequent interventions, contributing to the drop of the international reserve of Bank Indonesia by a conservative estimate of US$5–7 billion from July to October 2008, the Rupiah depreciated by as much as 23 per cent from August to October 2008. The downside risk remains high as foreign investors holds about 20 per cent of outstanding government papers at end of 2008.

INDONESIA

- The country experienced the worst meltdown of its stock market in 2008 and uncertainties are expected to last through 2009.

- Export and import dependent sectors will be badly hit, due to the slowdowns in the trading partners' economies and the volatile commodity prices.

- Liquidity constraint and high cost of financing will be the major challenge facing the domestic economy in 2009.

- The performance of the economy in 2009 and 2010 depends on the well-functioning financial market, successful elections and the recovery of the world economy.

Grim Outlook for Export and Import Dependent Industries

The economic slowdowns in the major trading partners of Indonesia is likely to hit the trade balance position from both the price and quantity side. Top four destinations of the country's exports, namely Japan (18.5 per cent of total exports), the United States (11 per cent of total exports), Singapore (10 per cent of total exports) and China (9 per cent of total exports), are forecasted to experience severe slowdowns. In the midst of the global economic downturns expected to continue well into 2009, the prices of the country's key commodities, including energy products, will likely to remain soft in 2009. In particular, the slowdowns in the U.S. and Japan should dampen the demand for the country's agriculture exports. At the end of August 2008, the exports to U.S. and Japan still grew strongly on year-on-year basis at around 30 per cent and 24 per cent, respectively. Yet, the August 2008 export numbers to Japan and the U.S. were about 24 and 9 per cent lower than their respective numbers for July of the same year.

Textile, electronics, wood, rubber and pulp industries are some of the key industries expected to perform poorly. In average, close to 70 per cent of the productions of the rubber and pulp industries for instance are targeted for the export markets. On the other hand, garments and textiles have high import contents and export-to-sale ratio, thus simultaneously exposing the industry to both weak demand and rising cost of production. Delays in the payments for the export-bound goods and cancellations of export contracts were already reported as early as October 2008. We still expect the current account to remain in the positive level in 2008, albeit at a significantly lower rate than its 2006 and 2007 level. International trade activities remain weak for 2009, but the current account balance should improve marginally. With the recovery of global economy in 2010, we should see the return of current account balance closer to its level in 2007.

Challenges Facing the Management of Monetary and Fiscal Policies

Strong surge in the inflationary pressure was a concern during the first half of 2008, but are expected to subside in 2009, largely due to the downturn in the global economy. The year-on-year growth of the consumer price index reached close to 12 per cent by July 2008. The strong inflationary pressure was largely driven by the unprecedented rises in the prices of key commodities, such as crude oil and food. The crude oil price raced to just below US$150 per barrel in June 2008 from around US$90 per barrel in December 2007. Similar rates of increase have been reported for the prices of key food staples such as rice, wheat and corn.

In response to the strong inflationary pressure, Bank Indonesia raised its policy rate several times in 2008, and the last one was by 25 basis point to 9.5 per cent in October 2008. Bank Indonesia (BI) was however blamed for the lack of forward looking policy and for being too late in responding — falling behind the curve. The credit of the banking sector had expanded in one year by more than 30 per cent in June 2008, fuelling further inflationary pressure. Despite the rising expected inflation, BI lowered its policy rate in 2007 and only started to rise it again in the first quarter of 2008. However the last increase of its rate in October 2008 drew even more criticism. While central banks around the world lowered their policy rates to support the weak demand in the economy, BI was the only central bank to hike its rate in the last quarter of 2008. With the slowdown of global demand, many argue that inflationary pressures should diminish together with the drastic falls in the prices of energy and food products, and hence require no additional tightening of the monetary policy.

In its budget forecast, the Ministry of Finance estimates that the rise of the crude oil price in the global market is expected to balloon the fiscal cost of subsidy from less than 4 per cent of GDP in 2007 to around 7 per cent of GDP in 2008. Already more than 50 per cent of the current expenditure of the central government budget has been allocated for mandatory spending, i.e. for debt service (or interest payment) and subsidy in 2007, this number is expected to rise by at least another 50 per cent in 2008. Given the sharp falls of the key commodity prices, the budgetary spending on the subsidy should moderate in 2009, and thus reducing the projected deficit for the year. However, given the parliamentary and the presidential election to take place in 2009, it is very likely that a number of populist policy measures will be introduced. In addition, counter-cyclical fiscal measures to support growth would be implemented in 2009. In turn, these policies and weak rupiah will fuel strong inflationary pressures in 2009.

Liquidity Constraint and High Cost of Financing

The cost of capital to finance investment in the local economy will certainly play a detrimental role on the short — to medium-term performance. In early September 2008, the Ministry of Finance (MOF) had to scrap its Rupiah bond auction due to the high yield that investors asked. The MOF had hoped to raise around Rp3 trillion (or around US$321 million at that time) from the auction of zero coupon and fixed rate bonds. The government offered around 9.5–10.5 per cent yields, but investors were asking for 13.5 per cent. The high asking bond yield reflects the rising credit risk as shown by the Emerging Market Bond Index (EMBI).

A failure to raise money from the domestic bond may force the government to sell foreign currency debt, which they did twice already during the first half of 2008. This however would expose the budget to volatile foreign exchange market. More importantly, the high risk premium for the government financing suggests even steeper borrowing cost facing the domestic private sector in 2008 and 2009. The high cost of borrowing has plausibly contributed to the cancelling of export contracts discussed earlier, as did happen during the 1997/1998 financial crisis. As a safeguard measure, the government of Indonesia had received from the World Bank a standby loan at around US$2 billion in October 2008.

Key Assumptions

The real GDP growth rate for 2008 is expected to be moderately lower than the expected official growth of over 6 per cent. Given the global economic slowdown would only be fully felt in 2009, a slightly lower than 5 per cent growth rate is forecasted for 2009. Only in 2010 that we should anticipate the return to around 6 per cent GDP growth rate. However, the downside risk with the economy remains high and the relatively optimistic scenario discussed earlier is based on the following assumptions. First and foremost is that the world recession will bottom-up in 2009 and we start seeing the return of stability in the financial markets around the globe. Second, we do not see massive collapses and bankruptcies in the domestic corporate and banking sectors. In particular, the banking sector must continue to function and to extend credits to the local businesses. Last condition is the smooth and successful parliamentary and presidential elections. It is very important that the implementation of credible and cohesive macroeconomic policies would not be compromised by the political uncertainties in 2009. The severity of the 1998 financial crisis in Indonesia, as compared to other affected nations in the region, was largely explained by the political turmoil erupted in the country. We do not anticipate a repeat of the 1998 political chaos, but a quick return of elected stable government is a must to ensure a steady economic recovery from the current global economic downturn.

Indonesia : Selected Economic Indicators, 2004–2010f

	2005	2006	2007	2008E	2009F	2010F
% change over previous year						
Gross Domestic Product	5.7	5.5	6.3	5.8	4.8	6.1
Household Consumptiom	5.0	4.0	3.2	5.1	4.5	4.8
Gross Fixed Investment	14.1	10.9	2.9	8.7	7.5	8.5
Merchandise Exports (f.o.b. US$ billion)	87.0	103.5	118.0	140.9	150.7	
Merchandise Imports (f.o.b. US$ billion)	69.5	73.9	84.9	112.7	122.6	
Current account balance (% of GDP)	0.1	3.0	2.5	0.6	1.1	2.0
Inflation/CPI average (% change)	10.5	13.1	6.1	9.8	9.5	8.5
Fiscal balance (as % of GDP)	−0.5	−1	−1.3	−1.3	−2.0	−1.6
External debt (% of GDP)	48.0	37.0	30	26	23	
Foreign exchange reserves (US$ billion)	34	42.6	56.9	50.0	57.0	70.0
Exchange rate at year-end (IDR/US$1)	9,711	9,167	9,139	12,000	9,500	9,000

NOTE: E is an estimate; F is a forecast.
SOURCES: Consensus Forecast, International Monetary Fund Database, Asian Development Bank Database, author's estimates.

Laos

Economic Performance

Gross Domestic Product (GDP) grew at 7.5 per cent in 2008, a slightly slower pace than in 2007. As in previous years, the engine of growth was foreign direct investments (FDI) in mining and hydropower. There are currently several mining and hydropower projects under-way (IMF 2008). One of the biggest hydroelectric power developments in Laos, the "Nam Theun 2",[1] has total investments of about US$1.03 billion (about 35 per cent of GDP in 2005). In the mining sector, the most successful development is the "Sepon Mining Project"[2] in the south of Laos. This project is operated by Oxiana Resources Ltd of Australia. Before 2002 agriculture accounted for about 50 per cent of GDP. This share declined to 42.3 per cent in 2006, and then to 38.6 per cent in 2007, due to the double-digit growth in the industrial sector. The average growth of agriculture was about 4 per cent during 2005–2008.

LAOS

- Laos has continued to enjoy rapid economic growth with improving macroeconomic stability.

- The resource sector has been the main source of growth, with investments in mining and hydropower projects.

- Growth is forecast to continue at a rapid pace over the medium term with inflation under control and a stable exchange rate.

- However, there are major challenges in the medium and long term, including macroeconomic management to effectively deal with the massive foreign capital inflows into the resource sector and policies to diversify sources of growth.

---

[1] For more details on the project, see Nam Theun 2 Power Co. Ltd at < http://www.namtheun2.com/ >.
[2] For more details on the project, see Sepon Gold Mine at < http://www.ozminerals.com/ Operations/Mining-Operations/Sepon-Gold.html >.

The service sector has grown by about 6-7 per cent since 2003. The growth of the service sector was the result of steady improvements in tourism and trade.

Inflation and the exchange rate have remained relatively stable. The Laotian currency, the Kip, depreciated about 0.1 per cent against the U.S. dollar from 2004-2005, but from 2006-2008, appreciated about 4.9 per cent against U.S. dollar. There are three main reasons for the Kip's appreciation. Firstly, the Government of Lao PDR (GoL) improved monetary and fiscal discipline to manage the exchange rate and control government spending. Secondly, there have been massive capital inflows from mining and hydropower projects. Thirdly, the U.S. dollar has weakened, as evident in its decreasing value relative to other Asian currencies. Appreciation of the exchange rate has led to lower rates of inflation. Inflation was about 6 per cent during 2005-2007, but is expected to increase to 13 per cent in 2008 however. The main reasons for the increase in inflation are increases in oil and international commodity prices and the expansion of broad money. Average broad money growth during 2006-2008 was about 30 per cent which was over the government's target of 10 per cent.

Laos fiscal balance has improved. The budget deficit as a share of GDP declined from 3.8 per cent in 2006 to 2.7 per cent in 2007, and is expected to decline to 1.7 per cent in 2008. There are two main reasons for the declining budget deficit. Firstly, the government has recently introduced policies to strengthen fiscal reforms, including implementation of a revised tax and customs law. Secondly, tax revenues have increased due to better tax collection management and increasing tax revenues from mainly natural resource tax income tax and profit tax.

Despite the expansion of gold and cropper exports, Laos is still facing a trade deficit.[3] The trade deficit is expected to increase from US$911 million in 2007 to US$1,144 million in 2008. The main reasons for the rising trade deficit are increasing imports of investment goods for the mining and hydroelectric projects. When these projects are fully operational,

---

[3] Here, we use data from international agencies which is different from official government sources. The GoL claimed Laos has had a trade surplus since 2007.

investment good imports will decrease, and mining and electricity exports will increase, which would lead to a decline in the trade deficit in the medium and long term.

The external debt burden remains high, at about 70 per cent of GDP during 2005–2008. However, according to an International Monetary Fund (IMF) projection, external public debt will fall. Most of the debt is to multilateral development banks and to the Russian Federation. Inwards FDI flows to Laos remained robust in 2007.[4] 2007 FDI inflows are estimated at about US$950 million, an increase of about 60 per cent from 2006. The growth of FDI was mainly because of a new large mining project (a new copper plant by Phoubia mining), non-resource industry investments and ongoing construction of three large hydropower projects (Nam Theun 2, Nam Ngum 2 and Xekaman 3).

Economic Outlook

Economic growth is predicted to continue, conditional on a number of assumptions.[5] The rate of growth will likely increase to about 8 per cent during 2009–2010,[6] due to contributions by construction activities in the new hydropower projects and mining projects, and expansion of their exports. The industry sector is forecast to continue to grow at double digits. Both the agriculture and service sectors will grow[7]; the former due to increases in FDI and the latter due to an increase in tourism and trade expansion. The number of tourists visiting Laos is predicted to exceed 1.7 million by 2010.

Under prudent monetary policy, coupled with responsible fiscal policy inflation and the exchange rate is expected to be stable in the

---

[4] Although the level of approved FDI has recently dropped (to nearly US$1.2 billion in 2007 down from about US$2.7 billion in 2006 (WB 2008).

[5] We make assumption that the government continues with fiscal reforms, State Owned Enterprises (SOEs) reforms, and banking reforms couple with continued prudent monetary and fiscal policy in order to maintain macroeconomic stability as the target in National Socio-Economic Development Plan 2006–2010 (GoL 2006).

[6] The impact of the global economic turmoil on Lao economy seems to be small because Laos has little direct link with global financial markets.

[7] The floods in Laos in 2008 had negative impact on rice production. However, rice production in the dry season seems to cover the loss of rice production from floods.

medium term. The inflation rate is expected to stabilize around 7 to 9 per cent. The Kip is expected to appreciate around 3 per cent against the U.S. dollar in 2009–2010, due to massive capital inflows from FDI, and general weakness of the U.S. dollar against Asian currencies. The trade deficit is expected to grow during 2009–2010 due to increasing imports of investment goods in mining and hydropower sectors. The budget deficit is expected to decline about 1.5 per cent during 2009–2010 because of the increase of tax revenues from resource sectors couple with prudent budget management policy.

Main challenges of development

There are two main challenges for Laos. Firstly, good macroeconomic adjustment is required to cope with deprecation of the real exchange rate. Massive foreign capital inflows, couple with expanding windfalls from the resource sector and external debt might lead to larger appreciation of the real exchange rate. This would adversely affect non-resource sectors, such as agriculture, and non-resource industry in the medium and long term. Secondly, continuing domestic reforms (especially banking sector and state owned enterprises) is required. Monetary and fiscal discipline should be more improved in order to maintain macroeconomic stability in the medium and long term.

REFERENCES

Corden, W.M. "Booming Sector and Dutch Disease Economics: Survey and Consolidation". Oxford Economic Paper 36, 1984.

GoL (Government of Lao PDR). *National Growth and Poverty Eradication Strategy.* PDR Vientiane, Laos, 2006.

IMF (International Monetary Fund). *IMF Executive Board Concludes 2008 Article IV Consultation with the Lao People's Democratic Republic*, 2008.

——. Available at < http://www.imf.org/external/np/sec/pn/2008/pn08109.htm >.

Kyophilavong, P. and T. Toyoda. "An Econometric Analysis of the Lao Economy — Simulation Using Macroeconomic Model —". In *Laos: Transformation to the Market Economy under a Single-Party Regime*, edited by N. Amakawa and N. Yamada. Kenkyu Sosho (IDE Research Series), no. 545, Institute of Developing Economies (IDE), JETRO, Japan, 2004.

——. "Macroeconomic Management of the Lao Economy — An Econometric Evaluation —". *Journal of Economic Sciences*, vol. 9, no. 1, 2005.

WB (World Bank). *Lao PDR Economic Monitor*. World Bank Office, Vientiane, Laos, 2008.

Laos: Selected Economic Indicators, 2002–2008f

	2005	2006	2007	2008est	2009est	2010est
GDP growth (% change)	7.1	8.1	7.9	7.5	8.0	8.0
— Industry sector growth (% change)	12.3	13.3	12.4	12.5	12.9	12.9
— Services sector growth (% change)	7.8	7.6	8.0	7.8	8.0	8.0
— Agriculture sector growth (% change)	4.1	4.3	4.5	4.5	4.0	4.0
Exports (US$ million)	684.0	1,143.0	1,203.0	1,516.0	1,790.4	2,114.5
Imports (US$ million)	1,270.0	1,589.0	2,114.0	2,660.0	2,894.1	3,148.8
Trade balance (US$ million)	–328	–446.0	–911.0	–1,144.0	–1,103.7	–1,034.3
Current account balance (% of GDP)	–17.8	–10.5	–17.4	–17.8	–17.1	–13.5
Inflation/CPI average (% change)	8.8	4.7	5.6	13.1	6–9	6–9
M2 money supply growth (% change)	7.7	30.1	38.7	38.9	16–19	16–20
Fiscal balance (as % of GDP)	–4.5	–3.8	–2.7	–1.7	–1.5	–1.4
Total debt outstanding (US$ million)	2,203.0	2,308.0	2,446.0	2,589.0	3,787.8	3,802.4
Long-term debt (US$ million)						
Debt service ratio (as % of exports)	57.9	48.9	110.8	75.2	21.1	24.4
Foreign exchange reserves (US$ million)	238.0	335.0	539.0	789.0	1,205.9	1,312.0
Exchange rate at year-end (S$/US$1)	10,137.5	10,136.4	9,560.0	8,735.0	8,473.0	8,218.8

NOTES 1: Author's estimation by consulting with economists in Ministry of Finance, Bank of Lao PDR and Ministry of Planing and Investment.

2: est refers to estimated values.

SOURCES: GoL (2006), IMF (2008), WB (2008), Ministry of Finance, Bank of Lao PDR.

Malaysia

2008 has been a difficult year for the world financial system as it faced the global financial crisis. This financial woes is something the world has never seen before in eighty years since the Great Depression in 1929. On 16 September 2008, the Lehman Brothers collapse has sent shock waves around the world. It is the biggest bankruptcy in history and also stands to become the most complex. Subsequently, Merrill Lynch was sold to the Bank of America, and American International Group (AIG) (world's largest insurance company) was bailed out. The Federal Reserve Board of the United States (Fed) stepped in and agreed to provide a two-year $85 billion secured revolving credit facility to AIG to ensure the company met its liquidity needs.

In the external front, the complexity of these derivatives led to much difficulty for global pricing and liquidation under market turmoil. The US$700 billion bail-out bill was immediately signed on 3 October 2008. On 12 October 2008, the European leaders in Brussels passed a 2 trillion euro financial rescue plan. Without these government actions, the collapse of AIG could have caused every other major bank in the world to fail.

The credit crunch has toppled banks in the U.S. and Europe, forcing governments to intervene and take stakes in lenders to prevent

MALAYSIA

- Malaysian Financial Story: Watching the impact of global financial markets meltdown on local markets.

- Prime Minister's Department and National Economic Council: Watching a rocketing of oil prices to a skydiving of oil prices amidst a pro-growth policy — 'Economic Stabilization Plan'.

- Mega Economic Corridors Projects: Review continued investment in Iskandar Malaysia, NCER, ECER, SDC and SCORE.

- Safe-haven from the Malaysia International Islamic Products: To spur further growth and position Malaysia as an Islamic financial hub.

any more collapses. The U.S. Congress in October 2008 passed legislation allowing the Treasury to spend as much as US$700 billion to buy troubled mortgage-related assets and purchase equity in banks. European leaders on 12 October agreed to guarantee new bank refinancing and use taxpayer money to keep distressed lenders afloat.

In Malaysia, the global financial bloodbath has spilled into differing degrees of impacts. On one end, the global crisis has destroyed RM75 billion of wealth from Malaysia's top thirty richest tycoons. By adding up the top three tycoons losses, based on the Forbes 2008, these losses amounted to a staggering 8.88 per cent of Malaysian's total real Gross Domestic Product (RGDP) of RM505.35 billion! On the other end, insurance companies like the American International Assurance Bhd (AIA Bhd), has not been impacted as much by the ongoing financial turmoil in the U.S. This was because more than 96 per cent of AIA Bhd's total assets are invested in Malaysia, and with a well capitalized balance sheet, the company was able to maintain separate reserves in Malaysia.

On the local front, the day after the global financial meltdown (17 October 2008), Prime Minister Datuk Seri Adbullah Ahmad Badawi and Deputy Prime Minister Datuk Najib Razak swapped the finance and defence portfolios between them. Najib taking over the finance portfolio was part of the power transition process between the two leaders. Najib is set to take over as prime minister in March 2009.

Bank Negara Malaysia (BNM), Malaysia's central bank, the Malaysian Institute of Economic Research (MIER) and the Asian Development Bank (ADB) all revised a projected Malaysia's growth to slow down in 2009, due to the weakening global economy. The official forecast for growth of Malaysia's economy in 2008, in gross domestic product (GDP) terms is 5.7 per cent. The official forecast for GDP growth 2009 is 5.4 per cent. BNM has forecasted the nation's economy to expand by as little as 4 per cent in 2009. On 15 October 2008, the BNM Governor, Tan Sri Dr Zeti Akhtar Aziz further stated that "... the next 12 months will be highly challenging, but the recovery could happen by 2010." However, the ADB projected a higher growth of 5.3 per cent, on expectation albeit of a continued softness in the external environment. But MIER projected a more lacklustre growth of 3.4 per cent in 2009, after growing 5.6 per cent in 2008. The expected lower real GDP growth in 2009 is projected based on less favourable natural resources prices, weaker external demand for manufactured goods and higher producer prices.

With the recent economic reports declaring Singapore already in technical recession, China's growth fell to 9.9 per cent in the third quarter of 2008, and a predicted recessionary Christmas for Australia (if interest rate is not cut by RBA), it is thus not surprising to see further gloom spreading over the Asian region. Demand for made-in-Asia exports will continue to weaken, as growth in the region's biggest markets are in the U.S., Europe and Japan. The International Monetary Fund recently forecast that the world's advanced economies will expand in 2009 at the weakest pace since 1982. Many economists also predict that should Organisation of Petroleum Exporting Countries (OPEC) pledge to dramatically cut oil production in the coming months, higher petrol prices per barrel could ensue, and this would prolong the world slowdown.

The rise in the prices of crude oil served as a double-edged sword for Malaysia. Malaysia benefits from higher crude oil prices because it is a net oil exporter. When the price was low hovering around US$30–US$40 in 2005, the government was able to subsidise fuel. Fuel subsidies amounted to RM1.7 billion in 2002. But in 2007, this amount jumped significantly to RM7.5 billion. Should the government continue to provide subsidies, this amount would surge to RM28 billion or constitute 5.24 per cent of real GDP in 2008, thus undermining fiscal sustainability.

On 21 May 2008, when oil prices breached the US$130 threshold, the government increased the pump prices of petrol and diesel by 41 per cent and 63 per cent, respectively. Following this, electricity tariffs were raised between 18 per cent and 26 per cent for domestic, commercial and industrial users. In July 2008, the inflation rate surged 8.5 per cent mainly due to higher food and fuel prices, marking its highest level since January 1982 when inflation was 7.6 per cent.

The government restructured the fuel subsidy system with effect from 5 June 2008 to curb leakages in the distribution of subsidies. On 14 June 2008, in order to reduce this increase of pump prices, the government introduced cash rebates of RM625 cash payout per vehicle, for private vehicle owners with engine capacities of up to 2,000 cc.

On 6 August 2008, a high-powered new economic council was formed in the Prime Minister's Department, to take on the role of an advisory body to tackle inflationary issues and a weak global economy. The council, chaired by Prime Minister Datuk Seri Abdullah Ahmad Badawi and Deputy Prime Minister Datuk Seri Najib Razak as deputy chairman, comprised ministers and representatives of the public and private sectors, mainly to assist the government in updating and coordinating policies and procedures to spur economic growth and overcome uncertainties.

Uncannily, the month of October saw a steep decline in the oil prices. Global crude oil prices started plummeting from a high of US$147 a barrel (7 July 2008) to US$71 (18 October 2008) a barrel in the span of three months. With the U.S. dollar expected to remain at its present level in the short term, a rally in oil prices stemming from a cut in production may push back prices at the pumps to as high as RM2.00 a litre. In that week itself, BNM made an announcement that the central bank will shift focus to boosting economic growth as inflation worries ease.

On 9 October 2008, Prime Minister Datuk Seri Abdullah Ahmad Badawi officially announced his decision not to defend his Umno presidency in the third week of March 2009, thus effectively giving up his premiership then. Making the announcement after chairing the Barisan Nasional supreme council meeting at the PWTC, he listed five initiatives, which he called his mission, that he intended "to see through" before leaving office. These are: (1) establishing the Judicial Appointments Commission to enhance the stature of the judiciary; (2) establishing the Malaysian Anti-Corruption Commission with greater powers of investigation and enforcement; (3) establishing the Special Complaints Commission to enhance the integrity and effectiveness of enforcement agencies; (4) strengthening and enlarging the Social

Safety Net to ensure aid to all, regardless of race and religion; and (5) holding a Barisan Nasional convention to improve inter-racial and inter-religious relations.

On 16 October 2008, the government announced the review and shelving of some projects including those in the economic corridors. These economic corridors are: (i) Iskandar Malaysia (Johor) — RM110 biliion expected investment; (ii) Northern Corridor Economic Region (NCER) — RM117 billion expected investment; (iii) East Coast Economic Region (ECER) — RM112 billion expected investment; (iv) Sabah Development Corridor (SDC) — RM105 billion expected investment; and (v) Sarawak Corridor of Renewable Energy (SCORE) — RM110 billion expected investment.

On 7 October 2008, Malaysia's single largest urban development to date, Medini, a catalyst development, was officially launched at the Cityscape, Dubai. This was part of Malaysia's long-term corridors objectives in Iskandar Malaysia. The launch of Medini is an important milestone, as Medini is Iskandar's first sizeable world-class offering to the international property space, and is expected to bring in over US$20 billion (RM69.6 billion) in gross development value over a period of fifteen to twenty years. This would mark the beginning of the unlocking of Malaysia's true potential to be a globally competitive nation. Medini is set to be a 920 ha international mixed-use urban development, located on prime greenfield land in the heart of Nusajaya (The World in One City), which lies in between Malaysia's second crossing to Singapore and the country's southern Johor State's New Administrative Centre.

It is expected that the government will bring fiscal consolidation programmes back on track after a slippage in 2008. Fiscal policy will continue to remain prudent in 2009, though expansionary, to support growth. Total Federal Government expenditure in 2009 is expected to increase to 4.4 per cent to RM205,899 million. The financing of the deficit is through Government bond issuance, and it could potentially be increased to about RM65 billion by 2009, from an estimated RM60 billion in 2008, as social and development infrastructure spending increases. It is expected that domestic liquidity will remain ample and bond appetite is likely to remain at around RM90 billion. Thus, it is projected that the fiscal deficit will widen to 4.8 per cent in 2008, from 3.2 per cent in 2007, before improving to 3.6 per cent in 2009. The focus of the recent Budget 2009 was on more "people-centric" projects such as low-cost housing, rural infrastructure and public transport. The budget deficit is unlikely to narrow significantly in 2009, given that social infrastructure spending is set to rise in the remaining two-and-a-half years of the Ninth Malaysia Plan (2006–2010).

On 20 October 2008, the government announced an "Economic Stabilisation Plan". The Deputy Prime Minister assured Malaysians to remain in confidence of the resilience of the Malaysian financial sector, and yet be mindful of the financial turmoil, as the Malaysian real economy will inevitably be negatively impacted. He outlined five steps to boost the economy: (1) to review foreign investment rules; (2) to liberalize the services sector; (3) to raise global competitiveness; (4) to tweak the budget deficit target; (5) to focus on projects that improve social safety net. The government announced that it would also inject RM5 billion to double the size of ValueCap Sdn Bhd. to support the Bursa Malaysia, the domestic bourse. Valuecap is a state-owned manager set-up in 2003 to invest in undervalued companies and stocks at a time when the global stock markets were worried about the effects of the U.S.-led war against Iraq. The domestic bourse has slid 37.1 per cent in 2008 as stock markets worldwide suffered the global financial crisis. Foreign Investment Committee (FIC) guidelines would also be reviewed to attract more foreign investors especially in property and commercial sectors, giving a preview of the measures to be put in place to cushion Malaysia from the impact of external developments. Other measures include Bank Negara's announcement to guarantee all deposits up to December 2010, and the strengthening of Small and Medium Enterprises and related financial institutions. The liberalization of the service sector, which was the main GDP contributor, would be detailed and based on a proposal by the International Trade and Industry Ministry to be proposed soon in Cabinet. On 4 November 2008, the Government projected its gross domestic product (GDP) growth for 2009 from 5.4 per cent to 3.5 per cent, but would inject RM7 billion to strengthen the economy and boost confidence.

The Ringgit has weakened after the global financial turmoil, slipping as much as 0.5 per cent to 3.5127 against the U.S. dollar. Overall, the Ringgit remained stable, following the strengthening of the major currencies against Ringgit during the third quarter of 2008. In particular, the strengthening of the Yen and the U.S. dollar is due to the unwinding effect of the carry trade, as investors liquidate their assets denominated in higher yielding currencies and switching back to the Yen and the U.S. dollar.

In terms of the interest rate policy, BNM has maintained its overnight policy rate at 3.5 per cent for 19 straight meetings, avoiding following its counterparts around the region in raising borrowing costs even after inflation accelerated to a 26-year high. However, due to weakening of the global economy, on 24 November 2008, the overnight policy rate was reduced to 3.25 per cent. According to Governor Tan Sri Zeti, BNM has the "flexibility" to move on interest rates if the growth slowdown warrants a cut in borrowing costs. Forecasting inflation to an average 5.5 per cent to 6 per cent in 2008, BNM foresees that the inflationary pressures would have receded as commodity and fuel prices decline, and consumer price gains may ease faster than initially expected. Should the inflation rate fall below 4 per cent before the second half of 2009, the balance of risks would be tilted towards growth.

Malaysian banks are still well capitalized, and have little exposure to toxic assets blamed for the global credit crisis. It is expected that "key" and "critical" lenders should continue to disburse loans to spur economic expansion. BNM will be ready to extend liquidity in the event of any tightening of liquidity conditions, should there be any disruption in access to financing. In a further notice, Bank Negara stated that it has no plans to impose new or tighter rules on Malaysia's financial system in response to the turmoil, as it had already strengthened the regulatory and supervisory frameworks in the past decade since the Asian crisis. However, BNM is prepared to take reforms, as market evolves, and new developments take place, the regulatory regime needs to be evolved to commensurate with these developments.

In terms of volume of trade, Malaysia's total trade value was US$323,115,984,770 in 2007. Malaysian's exports were valued at

US$176,205,639,147.00, and imports at US$146,910,345,623.00. Thus Malaysia still enjoyed a trade surplus of $29,295,293,524. The three top trading partners for exports are: (1) U.S.; (2) Singapore; and (3) Japan, and for imports are: (1) Japan; (2) China; and (3) Singapore. It has noted that the over-dependence on the U.S. market for Malaysia's exports has steered the trade policy to one of diversifying Malaysia's trading destinations to countries such as ASEAN and China. On this external balance, the trade surplus has helped Malaysia to further accumulate its international reserves of Bank Negara Malaysia to RM379.3 billion (US$109.7 billion) as at 30 September 2008. The reserves position is sufficient to finance 9 months of retained imports and is 4.1 times the short-term external debt.

Malaysia's foreign direct investment (FDI) outflows rose to 81.9 per cent in 2007, surpassing FDI inflows for the first time. Indeed this is a sizeable increase in outward investments, as it was driven by companies' cross-border acquisitions and expansion of businesses. The United Nations Conference on Trade and Development (UNCTAD), in its annual World Investment Report, announced that outflows of FDI from Malaysia rose to US$10.98 billion (RM38 billion) in 2007 from US$6.04 billion (RM21 billion) in 2006. FDI inflows increased 38.9 per cent to US$8.4 billion (RM29 billion) from US$6.04 billion in the same comparative periods. Among the top recipients of FDI inflows into South, East and Southeast Asia last year, Malaysia moved a notch up to 6th placing. Other transactions occurred included finance and other service activities like telecommunications and the extractive industries. Overall, Malaysian overseas investments have been rising in recent years, reflecting the ambition of home-grown companies engaging in international production. However, FDI inflows is expected to moderate in 2008 and 2009. The report also ranked the national oil company Petroliam Nasional Bhd (Petronas) 56th among the world's top 100 non-financial transnational companies (TNCs) in terms of foreign assets. Petronas was second, after Hong Kong's Hutchison Whampoa Ltd, in terms of foreign assets among the top 100 non-financial TNCs from developing countries. Other Malaysian non-financial companies from developing countries that made it into the list included YTL, Genting, Telekom Malaysia, Sime Darby and Maxis.

On the role of Malaysian Sovereign Wealth Funds, proactive government policies would be encouraged so that Khazanah Nasional Bhd could take on bigger financial stakes in the equity and bond markets. Khazanah Nasional Bhd has assets in excess of US$20 billion. Currently, Khazanah has a direct 51 per cent stake in Indonesia's PT Bank Lippo and an indirect stake in PT Bank Niaga via its 20.18 per cent stake in the CIMB group. On 30 September 2008, Khazanah Nasional Bhd managing director Tan Sri Azman Mokhtar announced that it is not rushing into buying foreign distressed assets created by the global crisis. Tan Sri Azman said the state-owned investment agency is instead adopting a cautious approach in its overseas portfolio amid mounting fears of a deep world recession. Khazanah has about 15 per cent of its assets invested overseas, the bulk of which is in Asia, insulating it from the worst of the financial turmoil. The agency's investment portfolio stood at RM53.1 billion as at 31 May 2008. Khazanah was a net seller in the twelve months leading up to June, booking RM7.8 billion of gains from five divestments and two monetization exercises via Islamic bonds.

Islamic finance in Malaysia is now one of the fastest growing segments of the global financial system with the *sukuk* (Islamic bonds) market in particular exceeding US$14 billion as of August 2008. It is expected to exceed US$200 billion in 2010. The *sukuk* market has also expanded at an annual growth rate of 40 per cent. This continued confidence of investors in Islamic financial instruments is a safe haven amidst a challenging environment, and will spur further growth to position Malaysia as an Islamic financial hub.

In any economic downtrend, domestic consumption is the main and first sector that would be most affected. However, this has not yet emerged in the Malaysian's consumption for vehicles. Malaysia's vehicle sales rose 12.8 per cent in September 2008 from a year earlier, led by demand for fuel-efficient cars. Sales of cars, vans and sport-utility vehicles climbed to 50,729 units in September 2008 from 44,984 a year ago. Passenger car sales rose 13.7 per cent to 46,476 units in September 2008 from a year ago. Local car-makers Proton Holdings Bhd and Perusahaan Otomobil Kedua Nasional Sdn Bhd, or Perodua, contributed most of the sales increase. Demand for smaller and fuel-efficient cars is increasing in Malaysia after the government raised gasoline prices by 41 per cent in June and diesel prices by 63 per cent. On the exporting front, the Naza Group of Companies, a Malaysian business conglomerate, which produces local cars under its own brand, as well as those of Kia Motors of South Korea, and France's Automobiles Peugeot, will increase it vehicles exports to fivefold in 2009. Naza can produce 50,000 cars in a year.

On a different front, Tun Dr Mahathir Mohamad, former Prime Minister, felt that the government has been underestimating the effects on Malaysia from the fallout of the global financial crisis. But he prayed that the government is right in assuring that the country is relatively insulated from what is happening to the global financial markets and the collapse of various financial institutions. The former PM pointed out that while Malaysia may not need "several hundred billions" to bail out the local banks, financial institutions will still face the problem of unpaid loans incurred by their credit card users, as unpaid credit card loans now amount to more than RM20 billion. In a similar note, Tun Mahathir added that Malaysia will soon face the problem of a shrinking market because up to 40 per cent of its exports goes to the United States and Europe.

Malaysia's economy should be able to tread through a world recession in 2009, provided that the world interest rates continue to decline over the long run. Should the global financial turmoil be further hurt by a second wave of credit crunch, for example due to a default of credit card payments, then an all increased interest rates policy would squeeze out all forms of real growth. In this scenario, Malaysia may not be able to weather this second financial storm as well as the first onslaught in October 2008. In many ways, the rest of the world and Malaysia's growth would depend on how the U.S. medium- and long-term interest rates farea. Should the interest rates go much higher in the next few years, it would add more bad news into the pipeline for the global financial system. A job that would be most daunting for Ben Bernanke or any central banker.

Malaysia: Selected Economic Indicators, 2004–2010f

	2004	2005	2006	2007	2008	2009	2010
GDP growth (% change)	6.8	5.0	5.9	6.3	5.6	4.0	5.0
— Industry sector growth (% change)	9.6	5.3	7.1	3.1	4.7	4.3	5.2
— Services sector growth (% change)	6.4	6.7	7.2	9.7	7.1	6.9	6.9
— Agriculture sector growth (% change)	4.7	2.6	5.2	2.2	3.6	3.7	4.5
Exports (US$ million)	126,511	140,979	160,676	176,161	187,977	199,756	214,908
Imports (US$ million)	105,283	114,625	131,153	146,901	158,071	168,655	182,709
Trade balance (US$ million)	27,572	33,156	36,698	38,119	39,461	41,608	43,278
Current account balance (% of GDP)	12.09	14.57	16.33	16.20	13.80	13.60	13.10
Inflation/CPI average (% change)	1.46	3.05	3.61	2.03	4.4	2.30	1.90
M2 money supply growth (% change)	25.2	15.6	17.1	13.00	15.9	9.20	6.90
Fiscal balance (as % of GDP)	–4.1	–3.6	–3.3	–3.2	–4.8	–3.6	–3.8
Total debt outstanding (US$ million)	52,155.7	51,980.7	52,525.7	53,384	56,936.3	59,384.3	63,081.79
Long-term debt (US$ million)	40,723.5	38,804.9	40,722.9	29,883	40,762.7	39,706.4	40,204.6
Debt service ratio (as % of exports)	—	—	—	—	—	—	—
Foreign exchange reserves (US$ million)	65,881	69,850	82,132	101,024	114,034.0	132,499	148,223
Exchange rate at year-end (S$/US$1)	3.80	3.78	3.53	3.31	3.45	3.55	3.40

SOURCES: Bank Negara Monthly Statistical Bulletin, Economic Report, The Economist Intelligence Unit and IMF *World Economic Outlook*.

Myanmar

As usual, Myanmar's GDP growth rate for FY2007 (ended 31 March 2008) has not yet been officially announced to the public. During the last decade, the average official growth rate of GDP was around 10 per cent; however, international financial institutions and analysts consider these figures overestimated. The government's Five Year-Plan (FY2006–FY2010) has projected an average growth rate of 10 per cent due to higher agriculture production, new gas fields and rising hydropower generation.

For FY2007, the International Monetary Fund (IMF) and Economic Intelligence Unit (EIU) estimated the growth rate at 5.5 per cent and 3.4 per cent respectively, largely due to growth in the oil and gas sector, teak and forest products, beans and pulses, rice, and mining products.

Positive and Negative Factors Influencing Growth Prospects

Let us look at the positive as well as negative aspects of the country's economy and attempt to forecast the growth rates for FY2008, FY2009 and FY2010.

On the positive side, export of gas and natural resources is rising and will boost the country's economy. The top trading partners are Thailand followed by China, Singapore and India. As far as export commodities are concerned, natural gas is the top export item, followed by forest products, fish and fisheries products, and agricultural products — mostly, beans, pulses and rice. In FY2007, Thailand was the largest importer from Myanmar with its strong demand for gas through the

MYANMAR

- The economy will remain weak in the earlier part of the forecast period and it will later increase slightly along with higher inflation due to the rising prices and the impact of cyclone Nargis.
- Export on oil and gas will continue to rise which will push up the GDP.
- New sanctions from the West and rising food prices will affect the cost of living.

Yadana gas field (20.1 per cent increase from previous year) and India, the second top buyer of natural resources such as agriculture (mostly beans and pulses) and forest products from Myanmar (5.3 per cent decrease) — not to mention smuggled goods — raised the trade surplus.

The growth rates of exports and imports increased in FY2007, 18 per cent and 9.4 per cent respectively. The trade surplus in previous year FY2007 was US$3206 million (EIU October 2008). It is remarkable that the export of natural gas accounted for about 40 per cent of total revenue of exports in the year FY2007. Myanmar announced its foreign trade for FY2008 was only for April and May.

Myanmar's neighbours, Thailand, China and India, are trying to compete among themselves to buy gas from Myanmar as they all strongly need energy. Meanwhile, South Korea and Russia also have some shares in Myanmar's oil and gas exploration. The following countries have investments (approved) mostly in oil and gas sector between FY2004 and FY2007: Thailand (US$6,080 million); United Kingdom (US$6,241 million); China (US$408 million); India (US$168 million); Singapore (US$166 million); South Korea (US$49 million); Russia (US$33 million); Japan (US$2.7 million) and Germany (US$2.5 million). For the FY2007, more than almost 80 per cent of officially declared FDI was directed into oil and gas developments. Recently in FY2008, China is running ahead in the energy race with more than 70 firms.

For FY2008 and the few next years, export revenues will be buoyant thanks to exports of natural gas from Thailand's strong demand. Because of the drastic impact of cyclone Nargis, export revenues have been affected and the agricultural, fish and fisheries and salt industry have less export revenues this year and probably for a few more years.

At the same time, imports have expanded since FY2001 due to higher foreign exchange reserves and stronger need to import building materials and equipments for major rehabilitation and reconstruction programmes after Nargis in May 2008. In 2007, the largest import items were machinery non-electric and transport equipment, refined mineral oil and base metals and manufactures (CSO).

On the negative aspect, the GDP growth is affected by price instability and the weak market exchange rate in the later part of 2007 and early 2008, and this resulted in low average incomes, less consumption and a lack of confidence. In addition, the impact of cyclone Nargis made the economy suffer severe damages after May 2008. There were 85,537 lives lost, 856,539 houses damaged, 1.3 million acres of farmland affected, 7,900 factories damaged, and transport and other infrastructure were severely affected. The total cost of losses from Nargis is estimated at 2.7 per cent of GDP.[1]

Moreover, the manufacturing sector was also affected due to the lack of capital, shortage of imported inputs, electricity and water and the damage to transport and other infrastructures. Taking into account the damage and losses and the expected rebound of the agricultural products in the fourth quarter of this financial year, the estimates of GDP for FY2008 would be 0.7 per cent. The economic growth rate in FY2009 and FY2010 would be around 3 per cent and 4 per cent respectively, due to recovery of the economy, particularly the rebound of agriculture sector.

Another constraint against economy growth is the official inflation rates in FY2008, FY2009 and FY2010 which was 39 per cent, 29 per cent and 13 per cent respectively, due to the surge in food and oil prices. If international aid agencies cannot afford to meet the required amount of food stocks, prices would surge much higher. In that case, "(the) central bank is set to carry on funding the government's budget deficit, and the consequent growth in domestic credit will continue to push up the general price level" (EIU, October 2008).

Regarding exchange rates in FY2008, inflows of cyclone-related international aid and remittance from relatives and other donors for the victims will prevent the Kyat (local currency) from drastic declines — evidenced by K1290/$1 before the Nargis to K1205/$1 after. However, it would affect prices when the exchange rate in FY2009 would remain on a long-term decline. In addition, it was found that there are poor prospects for consumption and for investment by local enterprises.

---

[1] Report prepared by the Tripartite Core Group comprised of Representatives of the Government of the Union of Myanmar, ASEAN and the UN with the support of the Humanitarian and Development Community.

Thus consumer spending will be constrained by low incomes and a lack of confidence because of price instability and the weak free-market exchange rate. At the same time, official exchange rates from FY2008 to FY2009 and FY2010 was K5.3/$1, K5.5/$1 and K5.5/$1 respectively.

Meanwhile, the amount of FDI declined from US$752.7 million in FY2006 to US$172.7 million (almost all in oil and gas sector) in FY2007 — a decline of 23 per cent — caused by political instability and new sanctions imposed by the U.S. and the West. The U.S. and the West added new sanctions in 2003, September 2007 and early 2008. This time the U.S. and EU sanctions targeted the assets of the country's leaders along with visa ban and tightening of exports and imports of Myanmar after the government's crackdown on peaceful protesters. Australia, New Zealand, Italy and Switzerland also added new sanctions. So far, no new investments from foreign countries have flowed into Myanmar during the period between April and May 2008.

Let us look at the country's business environment and trends. In FY2007, the tourism sector has been affected due to the violent crackdown on the peaceful protesters, including monks. Compared to the number of tourists in FY2006, that of FY2007 was only 78 per cent of the previous year. This was due to the governments of the U.S., New Zealand and Britain advising their citizens against visiting Myanmar. However, given the government statistics in the first quarter of this fiscal year, it seems that the tourism sector would slowly recover despite the impact of the cyclone.

As mentioned above, sanctions by the U.S. and the West extended to the foreign trade sector. Since the later part of 2007, the U.S. trade sanctions have blocked access to the U.S. financial institutions and there is tighter controls of exports of Myanmar's teak and gems and precious stones (Burma Jade Act), targeting specific crony companies, blocking the sale of rubies in U.S. routed through China, India and Thailand to circumvent or curb trade with Myanmar, and removing tax credits for U.S. firms investing in the country. Also, the sanctions stop Myanmar from using U.S. financial institutions via third countries to launder funds of the leaders or close relatives, while the offshore assets of the junta leaders have also been frozen. In May 2008, the U.S. again imposed sanctions on Myanmar, mainly three state-owned enterprises, the Myanmar Pearl Enterprise and Myanmar Gem Enterprise, and Myanmar Timber Enterprise.

The EU sanctions banned 1,027 junta-friendly firms in Myanmar and expanded the visa ban along with an asset freeze on its leaders — without harming the population. The sanctions target the country's key timber, metal and gem-stone industry and an investment ban on companies controlled by or linked to the government. It also prohibited export of equipment to EU countries involving timber, metals, minerals, semi-precious and precious stones as well as imports from these sectors. Switzerland also imposed sanctions on the import of teak, forest products, coal, metals and precious stones. Moreover, Switzerland banned financial transactions of owners of teak and metal industries from Myanmar. Italy has also boycotted gems mined in Myanmar; Australia directed its Reserve Bank to implement financial sanctions on not only the leaders, but also the owners of firms "favourable to the government".

As regards to the garment sector, despite U.S. sanctions imposed on the sector in 2003 and UN's Multi-Fiber Agreement (MFA) in 2005, export of garments earned US$282 million in 2007 because of global demand. About 30 per cent of garments were exported to Japan, another 30 per cent to the EU and the rest to Latin America. However, orders for new consignments have been reduced; it is expected that there will be serious impact felt from the global financial crisis by December 2008.

To conclude, the business trend in the country is not favourable for the period FY2009–FY2010 owing to the lack of conducive business environment — factors such as the increase of government intervention or self-imposed sanctions in the market, frequent changes in economic policies, restrictions in foreign trade sectors in the form of export taxes and controls on the type of goods to be imported, controls in private sector, and the lack of a "level-playing field".

In light of the above, the short-term outlook is not encouraging owing to recent international sanctions and stalled economic reforms. For this fiscal year and the next two years, the GDP is expected to slow down to 0.7 per cent (FY2008), 3.5 per cent (FY2009) and 4 per cent (FY2010) respectively.

Myanmar: Selected Economic Indicators

	FY2003	FY2004	FY2005	FY2006	FY2007	Estimate/Projection		
						FY2008	FY2009	FY2010
GDP(% change) (Official)	13.8	13.6	13.2	12.7	10.0F	10.0F	10.0F	10.0F
GDP(International Monetary Fund)	0.0	5.0	4.5	7.0	5.5	3.9	4.0	4.0
GDP (Economist Intelligence Unit)	-2.0	-2.7	5.2	3.4	3.4	0.9	3.0	3.9
— Industry sector growth (% change)	20.8	21.4	19.9	8.2	9.0	13.0	6.8	7.9
— Services sector growth (% change)	14.6	14.4	13.1	1.7	3.5	0.6	2.9	3.6
— Agriculture sector growth (% change)	11.7	11.0	12.1	3.0	1.4	-3.0	1.5	2.5
Exports (US$ million)	2,781.0	2,927.0	3,753.0	4,555.0	6,170.0	6,359.0	6,227.0	6,534.0
Imports (US$ million)	2,240.0	1,999.0	1,744.0	2,343.0	2,964.0	3,652.0	3,978.0	4,105.0
Trade balance (US$ million)	541.0	9,28.0	2,009.0	2,212.0	3,206.0	2,707.0	2,249.0	2,429.0
Current account balance (% of GDP)	-1.0	112.0	570.0	759.0	1,453.0	935.0	630.0	580.0
Inflation/CPI average (% change)	8.0	7.7	12.6	20.0	35.0	38.7	28.5	12.7
M2 money supply growth (% change)	11.0	32.4	27.3	27.2	30.0	22.3	22.5	22.7
Fiscal balance (as % of GDP)	-5.4	-1.9	-2.2	-2.6	-3.0	-3.5	-3.6	-3.6
Total debt outstanding (US$ million)	6,938.0	7,239.0	6,645.0	6,828.0	7,022.0	7,112.0	7,163.0	7,185.0
Total external debt (US$ million)	6,938.0	7,239.0	6,648.0	6,828.0	7,000.0	7,100.0	7,200.0	n.a.
Debt service ratio (as % of exports)	2.3	2.4	2.1	1.8	0.2	1.0	1.2	n.a.
Foreign exchange reserves (US$ million)	2,859.0	2,970.0	3,170.0	3,207P	3,240P	3,269P	3,301P	n.a.
Official Exchange rate (kyat/US$1)	5.8	5.8	5.8	5.8	5.6	5.3	5.5	5.5
Market Exchange Rate (Kyat/US$1)	1,095.0	1280.0	1,305.0	1,280.0	1,290.0	1,210.0	1,300.0	1,350.0

Sources: CSO, *Selected Monthly Economic Indicators*; Economic Intelligence Unit, *Country Report, Myanmar*, various issues.
IMF Report, *Myanmar*, September 2006.
ADB Outlook, *2007 Southeast Asia: Myanmar*.

PHILIPPINES

Like the other economies in the world, the Philippine economy is not "immune" from the adverse impact of the global financial crisis. This is because of increasing interdependence of the Philippines with the rest of the world, as seen in the openness of its trade and investment regimes, and increased reliance of domestic financial systems to global markets. As the crisis continues to unfold, the outlook for the economy in the coming months is going to be overshadowed by the weakening external environment. Since 2007, Philippine stock markets have seen large sell-offs on concerns over increasing sub-prime losses, deteriorating credit quality and slowing global economy. In offshore bond markets, there is also evidence of significant re-pricing of credit and liquidity risks since the turmoil intensified last year. Credit spreads for Philippine sovereign bonds have increased while capital outflows have accelerated. Obviously, the country's dependence on exports and the growing foreign participation in local capital markets makes the Philippines vulnerable to changes in global financial conditions.

Against this backdrop, GDP growth in 2008 is expected to remain modest at 3.9 per cent as the crisis weighs further on domestic demand. Although private consumption will benefit from falling prices (as average inflation rate is expected to fall to 7 per cent from 9.7 per cent in 2008), growth in consumption spending is going to be limited by weak disposable income and deteriorating labour market conditions

PHILIPPINES

- The Philippine economy will not be "immune" from the adverse impact of the global financial turmoil.
- Weak private investment will continue to challenge the economy.
- The services sector will remain a key growth driver, with sustained but slower increases in trade and transport, storage and telecommunications services.
- The Philippines needs to confront a number of policy issues critical to sustaining the growth momentum and coping with the growing financial sector strains.

(sum of unemployment and underemployment rates of 27.8 per cent as at end-April 2008). Remittance inflows, which sustained growth in private spending over the years, could slow, particularly if conditions in the United States (where 49 per cent of overseas remittances originate) further weaken. Counterbalancing the modest growth in private spending will be an increase in public consumption as the government implements counter cyclical measures to stimulate the economy. However, with fiscal consolidation still a priority this year, public consumption is expected to grow slightly by 5.3 per cent.

Weak private investment will continue to challenge the economy from growing above potential, particularly given the current environment of slow growth and low business profitability. The government has planned to increase capital spending in 2009 to support domestic investment, but it is unlikely that fixed capital investment will pick up strongly. In addition to increased risk aversion generated by the financial turmoil, investors are still deterred by concerns over the country's business climate, including the rising costs and wages and poor infrastructure in the Philippines. As a result, investment growth is likely to slow to 4.2 per cent, before picking up slightly to 5.2 per cent in 2010, when a gradual recovery in both global and domestic economies is expected.

On the production side, services sector will remain a key growth driver, with sustained but slower increases in trade and transport, storage and telecommunications services. Reflecting the continued volatility in global financial conditions, growth in financial services is expected to be sluggish. Business process outsourcing (BPO) services — which has become an important source of growth for services sector over the last five years — will moderate as well due mainly to weak economic conditions in the U.S., which accounts for nearly 90 per cent of total BPO exports revenue and over two-thirds of foreign equity in BPO industry. As a result, services will grow slightly to 5 per cent, well below its five-year average (2002–2007) of 7.1 per cent.

With continued strong support to agriculture (e.g., the vigorous implementation of FIELDS Programme on food security and sufficiency which was launched in 2007), agriculture sector is seen to grow by 3.9 per cent. This should offset the modest growth in industrial output (3.7 per cent) as both manufacturing and construction subsectors are weighed down by volatile oil prices, and by low capacity utilization rate (currently below 80 per cent) and lower export demand for manufacturing (e.g., industrial machinery and electronics). The expansion in industry will also be limited by slower activity in mining and quarrying as metal prices in global markets are expected to soften from recent highs.

As weakening global demand becomes more entrenched (decline in world GDP growth to 2.2 per cent from 3.7 per cent in 2008; and world trade growth falling to 2.1 per cent from 4.6 per cent in 2008, as projected by IMF), the country's external balances will generally come under pressure from rising import bills for commodities and slowing exports. Growth in merchandise exports, particularly electronics (which accounts for more than 50 per cent of export receipts), is going to slow markedly to 2.5 per cent from estimated growth of 5.3 per cent in 2008. However, volatile oil and commodity prices, despite the fact that they have eased relative to their previous peaks, will cause merchandise imports to further increase, thus creating a trade deficit of US$12.1 billion compared to its level of US$11.9 billion a year ago. Largely because of sluggish export growth and moderation in capital flows and remittances, the current account will generate a small surplus amounting to 1.6 per cent of GDP by end–2009. Reflecting this, the official reserves are seen to improve slightly at US$38.4 billion by year-end as the peso consolidates at PhP48.50 against the U.S. dollar.

Although food and fuel prices are expected to subside in the coming months, inflation rate will remain elevated in the short term (averaging 7 per cent from 9.7 per cent in 2008), which means that monetary policy stance is expected to be on a tightening side. Unless the downside risks to growth become more significant and the current financial strains deeper, domestic liquidity (M3) is not expected to ease further (projected growth rate of 10.7 per cent). Policy rates are also likely to remain unchanged from their current levels for most of the year. On the fiscal front, the government has reckoned to limit fiscal deficit at 0.7 per cent of GDP in 2009 and to narrow it further to

0.4 per cent of GDP by 2010. But owing to structural problems of weak tax collection and low tax-effort ratio, and the challenges of implementing stimulus measures to boost growth, fiscal difficulties will continue to prevail despite efforts to consolidate.

Moving forward the Philippines needs to confront a number of policy issues critical to sustaining the growth momentum and coping with the growing financial sector strains. First is the need to enhance domestic investment by increasing the contribution of domestic investment to growth. Since the 1997 crisis, domestic investment has been sluggish (19 per cent of GDP) and failed to contribute significantly to growth. To address this, it is important to continuously improve investment climate through policies that support investors. Eliminating key infrastructure bottlenecks is also needed.

Second, it is critical that the government continues to pursue the much needed fiscal reforms in the country. Tax effort has been low over the years (13.2 per cent), so there is an urgent need to reverse that slump by accelerating tax administration reforms. For example, at the Bureau of Internal Revenue, there is a need to strengthen taxpayer registration, arrears collection and improve on audits. In addition, measures to raise index excises, rationalize tax incentives, and reform other government-owned and controlled corporations should be the priorities.

Third, despite substantial progress in strengthening the banking system, a number of challenges remain to strengthen financial intermediation in the country. In particular, there is a need to revive bank lending growth which has been sluggish for a number of years. For example, bank lending did not recover strongly since 1997 compared to other countries in the region. Bank loans as per cent of GDP contracted from a peak of 58 per cent in 1997 to 26 per cent in 2008. Private lending has become conservative. In 2008, bank credit to private sector grew by only 4.5 per cent, one of the slowest in the region, compared to 37.2 per cent average growth registered in 1992–1996. Moreover, the balance sheets of the banks should be further strengthened. Although progress has been made in reducing non-performing assets, NPAs remain large and only 20 per cent of

Philippines: Selected Economic Indicators, 2004–2010

	2004	2005	2006	2007	2008E	2009F	2010F
GDP growth (%)	6.4	4.9	5.4	7.2	4.6	3.9	4.9
— Agriculture	5.2	2.0	3.7	4.9	3.7	3.9	3.8
— Industry	5.2	3.8	4.8	7.1	4.1	3.7	4.8
— Services	7.7	7.0	6.5	8.1	5.4	5.0	6.2
Exports (US$ million)	38,794	40,263	46,526	49,512	52,130	53,433	56,906
Imports (US$ million)	44,478	48,036	53,258	57,723	64,046	65,529	67,115
Trade Balance (US$ million)	-5,684	-7,773	-6,817	-8,211	-11,916	-12,096	-10,209
Current Account (% GDP)	1.9	2.0	4.5	4.4	1.5	1.6	2.1
CPI Inflation (average;%)	6.0	7.6	6.2	2.8	9.7	7.0	4.5
M3 growth (average; %)	10.3	10.3	22.7	14.3	9.5	10.7	11.8
Interest Rate (%; end-period)*	6.0	5.6	5.3	3.7	6.0	6.7	6.1
Fiscal Balance (% GDP)	-3.8	-2.7	-1.1	-0.2	-0.9	-0.7	-0.4
Public Sector Debt (% GDP)	95.4	92.6	81.9	71.8	73.2	66.9	66.2
Ext Debt (% GDP)	63.1	54.9	50.5	38.1	33.8	31.0	30.5
Reserves (US$ million)	14,560	17,659	22,953	33,751	38,233	38,450	39,959
Exchange Rate (end-period)	56.26	53.06	49.13	41.40	49.0	48.50	45.14

NOTE: * 91-day T-bill rate.
SOURCES: Country websites, IMF WEO, ADB Economic Outlook, EIU, author's estimates.

total NPA stock has been concluded. This caused the return on bank assets to remain one of the lowest in the region.

Finally, since the current crisis is all about fixing the financial systems, the Philippines should continue to focus on key critical areas that affect the domestic financial systems. There is an urgent need to address the increasing financial uncertainty and potential instability by enhancing transparency and governance, improving risk assessment, management and surveillance of financial institutions, and strengthening supervision and regulation.

SINGAPORE

As the global economy sinks into what is likely to be its worst slowdown in decades, Singapore, one of the most open economies in the world, is particularly at risk. Not only is its trade to GDP ratio of close to 350 per cent among the highest in the world, it is also exposed to global shocks through its considerable financial, communications, tourism and other linkages to the rest of the world economy. In particular, diminishing international financial flows will tend to undermine Singapore's large financial sector. Foreign investment inflows, which have been a critical part of Singapore's growth, are also likely to lose momentum and its port and airport will see declines in activity as well. Consequently, Singapore is likely to experience considerable turbulence in its economy in 2009. However, the unavoidable vulnerability that its openness creates is mitigated by Singapore's structural strengths which provide it with a greater capacity to bounce back from such shocks than its openness implies.

SINGAPORE

- Singapore is likely to experience considerable turbulence in its economy in 2009 but this is mitigated by its structural strengths.

- The government also has considerable resources to combat a slowdown and has a track record of swift policy responses to shocks.

- Large infrastructural projects, notably the integrated resorts, will also help to shore up growth during the forecast period.

CURRENT STATE OF THE ECONOMY

Economy already losing momentum

Figure 1 shows how the Singapore economy entered the global downturn with its economic momentum already decelerating. GDP growth fell sharply in recent quarters, with the third quarter of 2008 showing the first year-on-year contraction in five years. The lead indicator which provides a guide to the trajectory of the economy in nine to twelve months' time is pointing to further weakness. Figure 2 shows how that Singapore's exports to virtually all its major export markets contracted in August 2008 compared to August 2007 (when the global financial crisis began). Clearly, the lassitude in the global economy was already hurting Singapore's growth well before the sharp turn for the worse in the global economy in September 2008.

An analysis of the main components of the Singapore economy shows the vulnerability of the economy to further deterioration in the

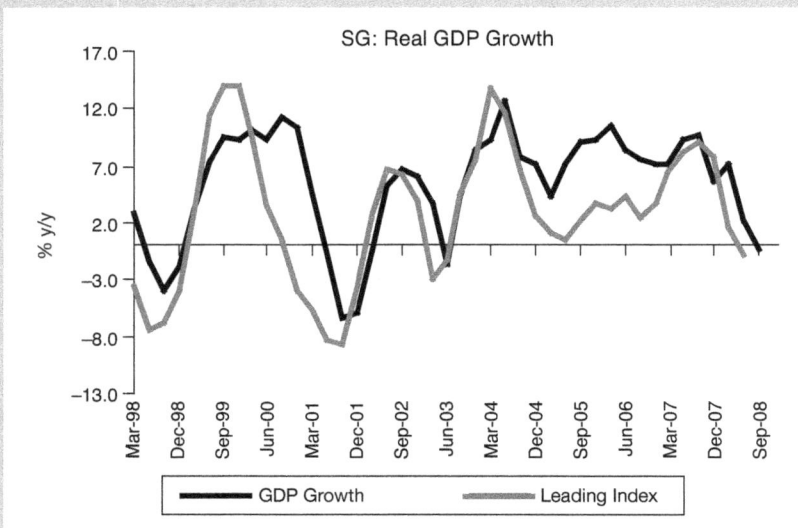

Figure 1: GDP Growth turned Negative, Lead Indicator Down

SG: Real GDP Growth

Legend: GDP Growth — Leading Index

SOURCE: Collated by Centennial Group using CEIC Database.

Figure 2: Collapse in All Export Markets

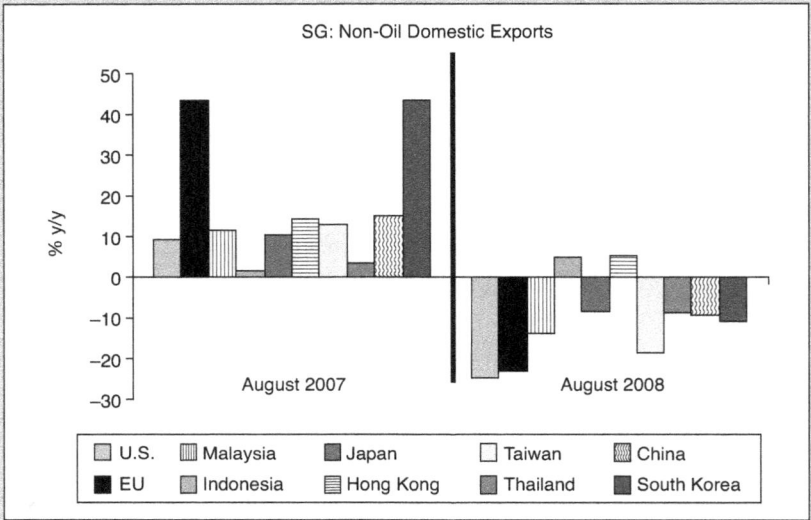

SG: Non-Oil Domestic Exports

August 2007   August 2008

| □ U.S. | ▦ Malaysia | ■ Japan | □ Taiwan | ▦ China |
| ■ EU | ▨ Indonesia | ▤ Hong Kong | ■ Thailand | ■ South Korea |

SOURCE: Collated by Centennial Group using CEIC Database.

Table 1: Analysis of Key Components of the Economy

Key Component of Economy	Assessment
Externally–oriented sectors	
Electronics production	Most sensitive to business spending on information technology in rich countries. U.S. data shows clear signs of future weakness.
Pharmaceutical production	Pharmaceutical demand is usually resilient to a slowdown but multinational companies producing in Singapore might choose to allocate production to cheaper facilities elsewhere.
Marine transport engineering	Driven by oil exploration activities. Susceptible to falling oil prices and credit crunch which is causing customers to default on orders and progress payments.
Global and regionally linked financial services	Singapore's foreign exchange and equity trading will suffer. Financial services to support regional growth (loan syndication etc) will also be hit.

Table 1   (continuted)

Key Component of Economy	Assessment
Trade–related services	Entrepot trade (import–export) activities and related support services in warehousing/distribution etc. will be hurt as regional demand slows.
Port and airport services	Falling cargo, passenger volumes will probably cause some contraction in these areas.
Domestically-oriented sectors	
Domestic bank loans	Mainly driven by real estate sector and personal consumption, both of which look parlous.
Construction	Already losing momentum, likely to slow further.
Real estate–related services	Fears of further asset price correction and growing economic uncertainty will mean reduced transactions volume in real estate.

global economy. Essentially, there is no major sector of the economy that is likely to escape the unfolding global downturn.

Economy also burdened by other problems

Prior to the global slowdown, Singapore had experienced strong growth which put a strain on resource utilisation. This led to rising costs — wages, rentals and costs of intermediate goods all rose. In response to this higher inflation, the authorities tightened monetary policy by allowing a faster appreciation of the trade-weighted exchange rate.

In short, Singapore went into the current economic turmoil with a high cost structure and a stronger currency, each of which was already slowing the economy even before the recent deterioration in the global economy. Figure 3 shows how unit business costs in manufacturing had risen significantly in recent years. Figure 4 shows the appreciation in the nominal value of the currency.

The economy was adjusting to these developments as the global shocks unfolded. Figure 5 shows how the construction sector slowed as huge increases in the cost of major inputs such as sand, steel bars, hiring cranes and other equipment all rose. The bottlenecks forced the

Figure 3: Rising Unit Costs in Economy

SG: Unit Business Cost of Manufacturing

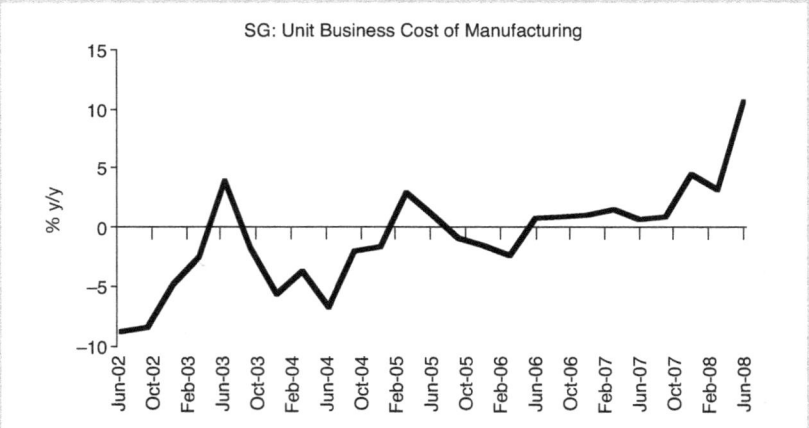

SOURCE: Collated by Centennial Group using CEIC Database.

Figure 4: Currency Appreciated in line with Policy

SG: NEER vs Estimated Policy Band

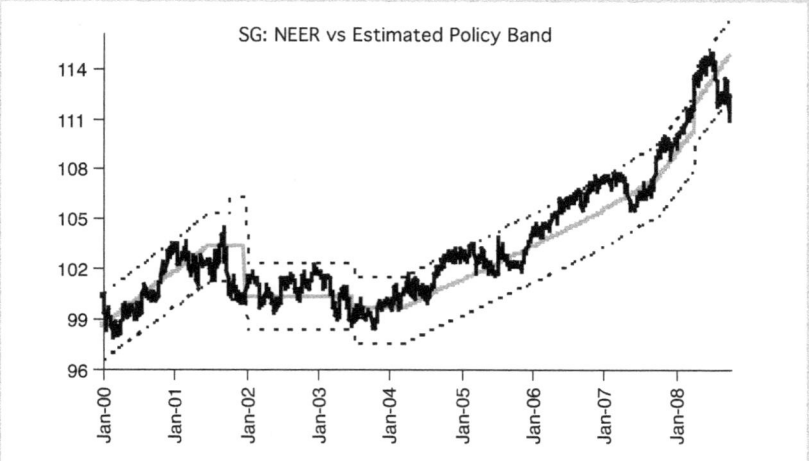

SOURCE: Collated by Centennial Group using CEIC Database.

government to postpone major construction projects as well. Figure 6 indicates how tourism, a sector sensitive to an appreciating currency, was hurt as well.

Figure 5: Construction Slowed as Costs Rose

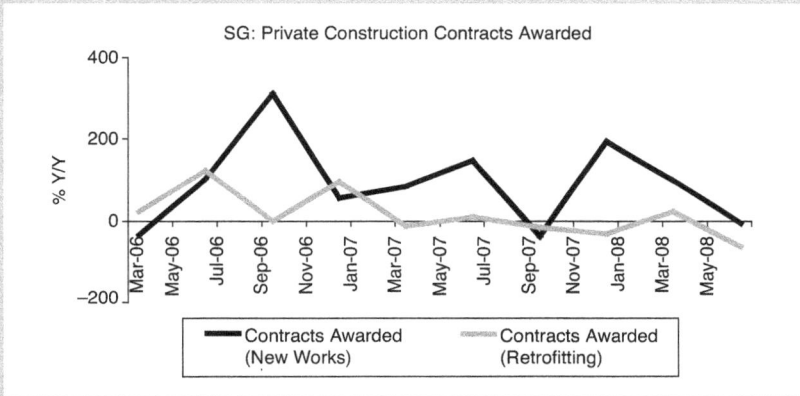

SG: Private Construction Contracts Awarded

Contracts Awarded (New Works) — Contracts Awarded (Retrofitting)

SOURCE: Collated by Centennial Group using CEIC Database.

Figure 6: Currency–sensitive Sector, Tourism, Weakened

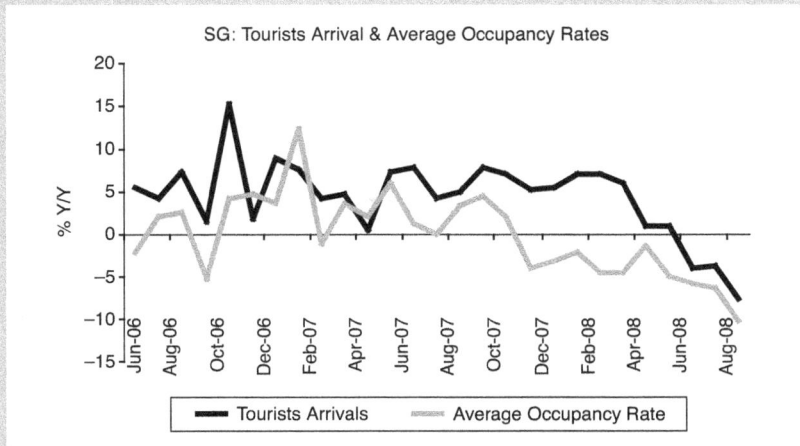

SG: Tourists Arrival & Average Occupancy Rates

Tourists Arrivals — Average Occupancy Rate

SOURCE: Collated by Centennial Group using CEIC Database.

How resilient will the economy be?

An economy that is as open as Singapore cannot avoid being buffeted by the storms in the global economy. As 2009 progresses, the economy is bound to experience further contraction in its major engines of growth. Not only will activities directly related to the global economy face some slowing but we will also see domestic sectors suffer. Local financial institutions cannot escape from the global financial turmoil which is causing lenders to turn cautious and cut credit lines. The heightened risks in the economy as well as tighter credit and the demonstration effect of falling real estate prices in major economies will also cause local home buyers to become warier. This will put considerable downward pressure on real estate prices in Singapore. A contracting economy, rising joblessness and falling asset prices could also raise the risks of higher non-performing loans in the domestic banking sector.

Moreover, as the economy endures a recession in much of 2009 at the same time as it is burdened by a higher cost structure, the economy will tend to adjust by forcing down labour costs, rentals and the costs of other non-traded goods and services in the economy. Added to the almost certain sharp fall in energy costs, we are likely to see prices falling through a good part of 2009.

Despite these ominous projections, we also see some mitigating factors that will lend support to Singapore's resilience:

- There are strong shock absorbers in the economy. External reserves are high, banks are well-capitalized and the corporate sector outside the property developers has been conservatively managed so their balance sheets are strong. There is little in the way of currency mismatches in external debt which is anyway low.
- Moreover, the government has considerable resources with which to combat a slowdown and has a track record of swift policy responses to such shocks. Recent constitutional amendments give the government more latitude in using the net investment returns from the country's massive stock of government savings for pump priming domestic demand. The government can now bring back into

Singapore: Selected Economic Indicators, 2002–2010f

	2002	2003	2004	2005	2006	2007	2008F	2009F	2010F
GDP growth (% change)	4.2	3.5	9.0	7.3	8.2	7.7	1.8	-2.9	4.5
— Industry sector growth (% change)	4.0	1.2	10.5	8.0	10.5	7.2	-3.7	-4.3	5.1
— Services sector growth (% change)	4.3	4.4	8.1	7.0	7.5	8.1	7.2	-2.4	4.3
— Agriculture sector growth (% change)	n.a.	n.a.	n.a.	n.a.	n.a.	n.a.	n.a.	n.a.	n.a.
Exports (SGD million)	223,901	278,578	335,615	382,532	431,559	450,628	466,400	452,408	506,697
Imports (SGD million)	208,312	237,316	293,338	333,191	378,924	395,980	427,658	406,275	463,154
Trade balance (SGD million)	15,589	41,262	42,278	49,341	52,635	54,648	38,742	46,133	43,543
Current account balance (% of GDP)	12.3	22.4	16.8	18.9	22.2	25.8	14.8	18.0	15.0
Inflation/CPI average (% change)	-0.39	0.49	1.67	0.47	0.97	2.1	5.60	-0.8	1.2
M2 money supply growth (% change)	1.9	4.0	8.9	5.2	11.9	20.4	10.3	2.2	8.3
Fiscal balance (as % of GDP)	4.2	6.2	5.5	6.8	9.9	13.0	20.0	-1.0	2.3
Total debt outstanding (US$ million)	n.a.	n.a.	n.a.	n.a.	n.a.	n.a.	n.a.	n.a.	n.a.
Long-term debt (US$ million)	n.a.	n.a.	n.a.	n.a.	n.a.	n.a.	n.a.	n.a.	n.a.
Debt service ratio (as % of exports)	n.a.	n.a.	n.a.	n.a.	n.a.	n.a.	n.a.	n.a.	n.a.
Foreign exchange reserves (US$ million)	78,839	87,894	102,920	114,857	128,092	146,941	176,329	185,146	194,403
Exchange rate at year-end (S$/US$1)	1.74	1.70	1.63	1.66	1.53	1.44	1.52	1.4	1.3

SOURCE: CEIC Database and Forecasts by Centennial Group.

play the large infrastructure projects it had postponed when the construction sector was overheating in early 2008. The government had also eased monetary policy in October 2008 shifting to a policy of zero currency appreciation.

- In addition, the economy's resilience is also aided by the large output generating projects that are likely to come on stream in 2009–2010. These include two massive integrated resorts, the first of which is due to open in December 2009 and employ about 17,000 workers directly and indirectly. There are also very large manufacturing projects which are under construction and which are due to start production — these include large plants in chemicals as well as in the alternative fuels segment.

Thailand

The Thai economy is forecast to grow at 0–1.0 per cent in 2009–2010, down from 3.5 per cent in 2008, due to declined exports and sluggish public investment.

After enjoying a vibrant export growth of 20 per cent in 2008, Thailand's export earnings are likely to turn negative in 2009 and ease to a low single-digit growth in 2010. This is owing to a slowing global economic growth and rising non-tariff barriers.

THAILAND

- The Thai economy is forecast to grow at a flat rate in 2009 and 2010 due to declining exports and sluggish public investments.
- The short-term economic outlook still hinges largely on global economic growth, political situation, budget disbursement and oil prices.
- Thai authorities have implemented fiscal stimulus and accommodative monetary policies to boost the economy.
- Thailand's economic fundamentals remain satisfactory with declining inflation, manageable public debt level and ample international reserves. Nevertheless, the airport closures in 2008 undermined Thailand's credit rating outlook from stable to negative.

Although Thai exporters have been successful in diversifying their markets away from the three traditional markets (the U.S., the EU and Japan), these markets remain the country's largest export destinations with a total of 35 per cent. In 2008, the U.S. market accounted for 11 per cent of Thailand's total exports, the EU market 13 per cent, the Japan market 11 per cent, the ASEAN market 23 per cent, and the North Asian market 19 per cent.

With the looming recessions in the U.S., the EU and Japanese economies in 2009–2010, Asia's export-led economies will grow at a much slower pace, if at all.

Beside the slowdown in the global economy, Thailand has to confront difficulties with non-tariff barriers imposed by its trading partners. The non-tariff barriers that are of particular concern to Thailand include rules of origin (RoO), technical barriers to trade, and sanitary and phutosanitary measures. Particularly, jewellery and the accessories industries have been facing problems with strict RoO from a number of importing countries.

To boost the Thai economy, a budget deficit target of 2.5 per cent of GDP has been approved for FY2009. According to the Finance Ministry, public consumption and investment are expected to expand by 7–8 and 8–9 per cent in 2009 respectively. The Thai authorities believe that accelerating public spending, especially through mega-projects investment, will have a crowding-in effect for private investments. However, the BOT expects public spending disbursement to fall short of the 94 per cent target in FY2009, as state enterprises lack an investment framework. Frequent changes in government administration have caused policy flip-flops and slow budget disbursements.

Private investment is forecast to grow at a near flat rate in 2009–2010, owing to persisting political uncertainties, sluggish public investments and a slowing global economic growth. Thailand's Board of Investment (BOI) reported a 20 per cent year-on-year drop in the value of new investment projects seeking its tax and privilege incentives during the first nine months of 2008. The BOI's survey in late 2008 indicated that major concerns of investors were local political risk, port strikes, the U.S. financial turmoil, reduced purchase orders from the U.S. and EU markets, and tighter regulations in financial markets. The BOI plans to restructure its incentives for some potential investments, and is considering more aggressive campaigns in new markets such as Russia, China, the Middle East and Latin America.

Private consumption growth is expected to remain low at 2.0–3.0 per cent in 2009–2010. Although consumer confidence has been deteriorated due to prolonged political unrest, declining inflationary pressures and moderate farm income growth would be positive factors on consumer spending.

According to the Bank of Thailand (BOT), inflation is projected to decline from 6.0 per cent in 2008 to 3.0–4.0 per cent in 2009, as global economic recession could lead to lower oil and commodity prices.

Overall, Thailand's short-term economic outlook still hinges largely on global economic growth, the political situation, budget disbursement and oil prices.

Regardless which political party wins the majority in the Parliamentary seats, it can be expected that the government would focus on domestic demand stimulus packages. Meanwhile, the central bank's concern has more to do with inflation and baht stability than with the country's growth.

In 2008, the government announced a number of stimulus measures. The tax stimulus package, approved by the Cabinet in March 2008, was to help relieve the tax burden on individuals, SMEs and listed companies in the stock market. In addition, the package also includes tax incentives for private investment and the real estate sector. The Finance Ministry estimated that tax burden, which would be alleviated by this package, was about 42 billion baht in 2008–2009. Later, in April 2008, the Cabinet approved funding schemes including a three-year debt moratorium for farmers and lower interest rate loans from the Government Housing Bank for small businesses. Under these schemes, government injection was estimated at 732.4 billion baht over 2008–2010.

In addition, the Somchai administration issued six new stimulus measures worth 1.2 trillion baht in order to cushion the country from the impact of the global financial crisis. The measures included an extension of tax privileges for retirement mutual funds (RMF) and long-term equity funds (LTF) investments from 500,000 baht to 700,000 baht a year, the use of the Stock Exchange of Thailand's initiated Matching Funds as a tool in accommodating foreign investors' sell-out, boosting of liquidity by the BOT at about one trillion baht along with the support for all commercial banks to approve more loans, stimulation of export and tourism revenues by at least 5 per cent, and timely budget disbursement which was set to be 180 billion baht more than in the last fiscal year.

With the stimulus measures, the Cabinet approved a 1.095 trillion baht public debt for the FY2009 budget. The government set a 4 per cent economic growth target for 2009. The Finance Ministry has confidence that the country's public debt level will be manageable. Total outstanding public debt was at 3.37 trillion baht at the end of July 2008, accounting for 35.8 per cent of GDP.

On financial stability, corporate sector's profitability and households' ability to service debt remained satisfactory in the first half of 2008. At the same time, non-performing loans (NPLs) have declined. Households' costs of living and costs of firms' production have tended to decline along with declining inflation. Households and businesses, however, would face higher risks from global economic downturn and fragile domestic demand. These may lead to an increase in financial institutes' NPL ratio.

Thai commercial banks exhibited high financial stability. The overall capital to risk-weighted asset ratio in September 2008 was at 15.33 per cent, higher than the 8.5 per cent minimum requirement by the BOT. Tier-1 capital represented 11.97 per cent to risk-weighted assets, or 2.8 times of the BOT's minimum requirement. In addition, there is high liquidity in the Thai banking system, indicated by their investments into BOT bonds which can be liquidated quickly. On the other hand, Thai commercial banks have small exposure to foreign liabilities and assets. These suggest that the financial sector was sound enough to withstand some higher risks posted by the country's economic slowdown and volatile global financial system going forward.

Regarding external stability, current account balance is forecast to turn negative in 2009–2010 due to a sharp decline in exports. Import value is predicted to decrease by 5.5 per cent in 2009 and turn into a positive growth of 9.0 per cent in 2010, down from 28.1 per cent in 2008. This would be owing to lower oil prices, together with slowing export and domestic demand. Net trade in services is expected to decline sharply in 2009 due to unending political conflict and looming global recession. Preliminary estimates by various agencies indicate that the one-week closure of Suvarnabhumi and Don Mueang international airports in late 2008 cost about 200 billion baht in losses to tourism, aviation, air cargo business and other related industries. The impact is expected to linger into 2009.

Foreign direct investment is likely to drop in 2009–2010 due to persisting political and policy uncertainty, and a slowdown in the key investing partners of Thailand, particularly Japan, Singapore, China, the EU and the U.S. Capital outflows may increase sharply if the market rescue programmes implemented by the U.S. and Europe are not successful in reviving confidence.

Thailand's international reserves are projected to decline slightly in 2009–2010 due to the current account deficit. International reserves stood at US$106.3 billion at the end of November 2008, increased from US$87.6 billion at the end of 2007. With strong international reserves, the baht is expected to remain stable at 36 baht per US$1 in 2009–2010.

In all, Thailand's economic fundamentals remain satisfactory with declining inflation, manageable public debt level and ample international reserves. Nevertheless, the airport closures in 2008 undermined Thailand's credit rating outlook from stable to negative. The country's short-term economic outlook would face both internal and external challenges. In line with the continued global economic slowdown and persisting domestic political instability, both exports and public investments would be weak engines of the country's growth.

Thailand: Selected Economic Indicators, 2004–2010f

	2004	2005	2006	2007	2008E	2009F	2010F
GDP growth (% change)	6.3	4.5	5.1	4.8	3.5	0.0	1.0
— Industry sector growth (% change)	8.0	5.4	5.8	5.6	4.0	-0.5	0.7
— Services sector growth (% change)	6.9	5.0	4.8	4.2	3.2	0.3	1.2
— Agriculture sector growth (% change)	-2.4	-1.9	3.8	4.0	2.9	0.5	1.5
Exports (US$ billion)	94,941	109,362	127,941	150,048	180,058	166,553	173,216
Imports (US$ million)	93,481	117,616	126,947	138,476	177,388	167,632	182,719
Trade balance (US$ million)	1,460	-8,254	994	11,572	2,670	-1,078	-9,503
Current account balance (% of GDP)	1.7	-4.4	1.1	6.0	-0.8	-2.5	-3.5
Inflation/CPI average (% change)	2.7	4.5	4.7	2.3	6.0	0.8	1.0
M2 money supply growth (% change)	5.7	6.3	6.2	1.2	0.2	0.5	1.0
Fiscal balance (as % of GDP)	0.3	0.2	0.1	-1.1	-1.7	-2.5	-3.0
Total debt outstanding (US$ million)	51,312	52,039	59,643	61,738	68,000	72,000	73,000
Long-term debt (US$ million)	39,138	35,631	41,089	40,097	40,903	44,640	45,260
Debt service ratio (as % of exports)	8.5	10.8	11.3	11.8	6.1	8.5	9.5
International reserves (US$ million)	49,832	52,066	66,985	87,455	102,000	90,000	85,000
Exchange rate at year-end (Baht/US$1)	39.1	41.0	36.0	33.7	35.5	36.0	36.0

SOURCE: National Economic and Social Development Board, Bank of Thailand, Ministry of Finance and author's estimation.

VIETNAM

Vietnam is a developing country that has spent the last twenty years or so undergoing gradual economic transition, away from central planning, and towards a more market-oriented economy 'with socialist characteristics'. The first seeds of this economic transition process began in 1979, and were concretized under the banner of 'doi moi' (renovation) at the 6th Party Congress in late 1986. The basic thrust of Vietnam's economic reform and business liberalization process has been fairly consistent over the last two decades, although not as emphatic as some observers would like. In return, the country has been rewarded with robust GDP growth, averaging in excess of 7.5 per cent per annum over the last decade. The aim is to become a middle-income industrialized country by 2020.

In the first nine months of 2008, Vietnam's policy-makers wrestled with an economy that was over-heating, as evidenced by high inflation

VIETNAM

- High inflation and a large trade deficit resulted in a mild case of home-grown financial instability for Vietnam in mid-2008, after a long period of sustained economic growth and stability. By the time inflation and the balance of payments were back under control, Vietnam's policy-makers had to gird themselves for an impending global economic downturn in 2009–2010 which will impact the country in a number of ways.

- Economic growth is likely to slow in 2009–2010. Burgeoning inflows of foreign direct investment (FDI) and portfolio investment will lessen, and foreign exchange earnings from exports will also grow more modestly than in previous years. The domestic corporate and banking sectors will struggle with a less benign economic environment, having become bloated in recent years of rapid growth. Getting the corporate sector on a firmer and leaner footing will be a policy priority in 2009–2010.

- Sizable ODA inflows and overseas Vietnamese remittances will serve as a useful economic cushion, as private sector growth weakens in tandem with the global economic backdrop. Credit will become scarcer, and various asset classes — including the equity market — will be range-bound. But social and political stability will be maintained, and economic reform momentum will remain broadly intact.

and a widening trade deficit. Monetary tightening measures were used to rein-in excessive lending growth by commercial banks, and state-owned enterprises were told to reduce their investment activity in non-core areas of business. By September 2008, these policy measures were beginning to have some traction, with inflation peaking at around 28 per cent, interest rates on loans at 21 per cent and interest rates on deposits at around 18 per cent. Fears in Spring 2008 that Vietnam would have a balance of payments crisis dissipated over the summer, as imports were brought under control and foreign exchange reserves did not drop below US$20 billion. Official figures suggest that crucial foreign direct investment inflows grew in 2008, despite a general rise in inputs costs (resulting from inflation) and an up-tick in labour unrest (also resulting from inflation). Nonetheless, Vietnam's reputation for having a stable macroeconomic environment took a knock in 2008.

Looking into 2009 and 2010, Vietnam is girding itself for a much more challenging global economic backdrop, which will probably result in a number of adverse impacts on the domestic economy. Export growth may persist, but at a much lower pace, and the earnings derived will weaken as the price of various goods and commodities lessen. Foreign direct investment (FDI) inflows are also expected to decline, as multinational enterprises scale back their plans for capacity expansion, and the availability of credit to help fund such projects becomes scarcer. Indeed, a number of large-scale FDI projects announced in 2008 may not proceed as planned. Vietnam's first oil refinery, located at Dung Quat in the central region, is expected to be commissioned in late 2009. This should help mitigate Vietnam's import bill, to some extent at least, as the country starts to refine some of its offshore crude oil production. (In 2008, Vietnam went from being a net exporter of oil to a net importer, as rising demand for petroleum has outpaced production.)

Even if private capital inflows to Vietnam contract in 2009 and 2010, inflows of ODA funding and inward remittances by overseas Vietnamese should remain fairly constant, thereby providing a useful financial buffer as the country charts its way through some stormy global waters. ODA assistance from Vietnam's development partners is likely to shift its emphasis towards more infrastructural support, and away from technical assistance in the regulatory sphere. In recent years Vietnam has done a commendable job in putting a lot of the regulatory framework in place to support a benign enabling environment for business, partly to support domestic business liberalization and meet the conditions set for WTO entry. But with ports, roads, power stations and various utilities now straining under rapidly growing demand from burgeoning industry and urban residents, there is a threat that future growth could be constrained if investment in physical infrastructure is not stepped up.

Vietnam's long drawn-out divestment of state-owned enterprises, known as 'equitization', failed to accelerate in 2008, due in part to the substantial drop in the value of equities — and some other asset classes — in the first half of the year. With the stock market floundering, there was an understandable reluctance by the bigger state enterprises to enact initial public offerings at low valuations. But there is a need to press ahead with what is perhaps the single largest missing component of the economic reform and business liberalization process in Vietnam — transforming the state corporations into more commercial organizations, operating on a level playing field with the private sector. Privileged access to cheap finance has allowed some of the larger state enterprises to develop 'keiretsu-like' tentacles into a wide spectrum of tangential (and non-strategic) business ventures, some of which could 'crowd out' the fledgling private sector. While the sale of some shares in these state enterprises will not automatically bring about more focused and sustainable business strategies for these corporations, it should be beneficial in a number of ways. If foreign strategic investors are also permitted to take (not insubstantial) equity stakes in these corporations, this could do much to improve the professional skills and expertise of the state enterprise sector.

As Vietnam progresses with its economic reform programme, the low-hanging fruit of transition become less and less. Arguably, the next phrase in Vietnam's economic development trajectory involves making the graduation from developing to middle-income economy. That in turn places increasing emphasis on creating and maintaining the institutions

Vietnam: Selected Economic Indicators, 2004–2010f

	2004	2005	2006	2007	2008	2009	2010
GDP growth (% change)	7.8	8.4	8.2	8.5	6.2	5.3	6.1
— Industry sector growth (% change)	10.3	10.7	10.4	10.6	7.0	7.0	9.0
— Services sector growth (% change)	7.3	8.5	8.3	8.7	6.6	4.6	4.7
— Agriculture sector growth (% change)	4.4	4.0	3.4	3.4	3.5	3.0	2.0
Exports (US$ billion)	26.5	32.4	39.8	48.6	66.5	72.7	85.1
Imports (US$ billion)	28.8	34.9	42.6	58.9	80.3	83.9	94.0
Trade balance (US$ billion)	–2.3	–2.4	–2.8	–10.4	–13.8	–11.3	–8.9
Current account balance (% of GDP)	–2.0	–1.0	–0.1	–8.0	–13.5	–7	–6.8
Inflation/CPI average (% change)	7.8	8.3	7.4	9.0	24.9	14.0	9.6
M2 money supply growth (% change)	31.1	30.9	29.7	49.1	12.3	27.3	20.5
Fiscal balance (as % of GDP)	0.9	–1.2	–0.3	–1.6	–1.7	–2.3	–2.3
Total debt outstanding (US$ billion)	18.0	19.2	20.2	21.8	23.8	24.3	25.3
Debt service ratio (as % of exports)	53.5	46.9	40.1	34.5	29.2	27.5	24.5
Foreign exchange reserves (US$ billion)	6.3	8.6	13.4	22.0	20.0	23.0	25.0
Exchange rate at year-end (S$/US$1)	15,777	15,916	16,054	16,030	16,806	17,129	17,429

Sources: EIU, BMI and ADB.

needed to support that drive. Hence, capacity-building in government, the state enterprise sector and the private sector are important priorities for Vietnam in the coming years. Public administration reform is needed in most areas of government. Improved corporate governance practices are required in most state-owned enterprises. And the private sector needs to make major strides in developing more sustainable business practices. With more than 1.5 million young people joining the labour force each year in Vietnam, there is little option but to pursue an industrialization approach to economic development, but in a way that does not inflict too much damage on the country's environment and unique biodiversity. A spate of corporate pollution scandals, involving both local- and foreign-owned companies, served to underline the risks posed in this regard.

At the time of writing, Vietnam's long-term sovereign rating by Standard & Poor's was BB+, BB- by Fitch, and Ba3 by Moody's. All three ratings agencies currently give a negative outlook for Vietnam. In the most recent iteration of the World Bank's 'Doing Business' annual survey, Vietnam ranked 92nd out of 181 countries. In the Fraser Institute's 'Economic Freedom of the World Exercise', Vietnam ranks joint 108th (out of 140 countries), along with Bangladesh. In the World Competitiveness Index for 2008–2009, Vietnam ranks 70th, and 121st (out of 180) in Transparency International's 2008 Corruption Perceptions Index.

THE CONTRIBUTORS

Political Outlook

Tim Huxley is Executive Director of the International Institute for Strategic Studies — Asia, based in Singapore. He contributed the section "Southeast Asia's Security Outlook".

Rodolfo C. Severino is head of the ASEAN Studies Centre in the Institute of Southeast Asian Studies and a former ASEAN Secretary-General. He contributed the section "ASEAN: New Charter, New Optimism".

Satu P. Limaye is Director of the East-West Center in Washington D.C. He contributed the section "United States-Southeast Asia Relations".

Andrew Symon is a Singapore based senior associate of Cambridge Energy Research Associates (CERA) of the U.S. He contributed the section "Southeast Asia's Quest for Energy Security: Cooperation and Tensions".

Pushpa Thambipillai teaches at the University of Brunei Darussalam. She contributed the country section on Brunei Darussalam.

Sophal Ear is an Assistant Professor in the Department of National Security Affairs at the U.S. Naval Postgraduate School, Monterey, California, USA. He contributed the country section on Cambodia.

Bernhard Platzdasch is a Visiting Research Fellow at the Institute of Southeast Asian Studies. He contributed the country section on Indonesia.

Martin Stuart-Fox is Professor Emeritus at the University of Queensland. He contributed the country section on Laos.

Johan Saravanamuttu is a Senior Visiting Fellow at the Institute of Southeast Asian Studies. He contributed the country section on Malaysia.

Robert H. Taylor is the author of *The State in Myanmar* (2008). He contributed the country section on Myanmar.

Felipe B. Miranda is Professor of Political Science at the University of the Philippines (Diliman). He contributed the country section on the Philippines.

Terence Chong is Fellow at the Institute of Southeast Asian Studies. He contributed the country section on Singapore.

Supinya Klangnarong is a media advocate and lecturer based in Bangkok and vice-chair of the Campaign for Popular Media Reform (CPMR). She contributed the country section on Thailand.

David Koh is Senior Fellow at the Institute of Southeast Asian Studies. He contributed the country section on Vietnam.

Economic Outlook

Sanchita Basu Das is Associate Fellow at the Institute of Southeast Asian Studies. She contributed the section "Regional Economic Outlook".

Omkar Lal Shrestha is Visiting Senior Research Fellow at the Institute of Southeast Asian Studies. He contributed the section "Regional Economic Outlook".

Razeen Sally is Director of the European Centre for International Political Economy in Brussels, and on the faculty of the London School of Economics. He contributed the section "The World Trading System and Southeast Asia: Emerging Protectionism and Post-Doha Challenges".

Melanie S. Milo is Fellow at the Institute of Southeast Asian Studies. She contributed section "APEC at 20: Retrospect and Prospect."

Aekapol Chongvilaivan is Fellow at the Institute of Southeast Asian Studies. He contributed the section "Food Crisis in Southeast Asia: What Caused? What Next?"

Aparna Bhagirathy Krishnan is Research Associate at the Institute of Southeast Asian Studies. She contributed the section "Income Inequalities in Southeast Asia: Potential for Microfinance".

Lee Poh Onn is Fellow at the Institute of Southeast Asian Studies. He contributed the country section on Brunei Darussalam.

Jayant Menon is Principal Economist, Office for Regional Economic Integration, at the Asian Development Bank. He contributed the country section on Cambodia.

Reza Siregar is Senior Lecturer, Adjunct Faculty, School of Economics, University of Adelaide, South Australia, Australia. He contributed the country section on Indonesia.

Kyophilavong Phouphet is Deputy Director, Department of Economics, Faculty of Economics and Business Management, at the National University of Laos. He contributed the country section on Laos.

Kian-Teng Kwek is Associate Professor, Department of Economics, Faculty of Economics and Administration, University of Malaysia. She contributed the country section on Malaysia.

Mya Than is Associate Senior Fellow at the Institute of Southeast Asian Studies. He contributed the country section on Myanmar.

Aladdin D. Rillo is International Consultant (Macroeconomist) at the Asian Development Bank. He contributed the country section on Philippines.

Manu Bhaskaran is Partner/Head, Economic Research, Centennial Group Holdings. He contributed the country section on Singapore.

Sakulrat Montreevat is Senior Researcher at the Fiscal Policy Research Institute, Thailand. She contributed the country section on Thailand.

Nick J. Freeman is an independent economic development consultant, resident in Vietnam, and an Associate Senior Fellow of the Institute of Southeast Asian Studies. He contributed the country section on Vietnam.

THE EDITORS

Ian J. Storey is Fellow at the Institute of Southeast Asian Studies.

Lee Poh Onn is Fellow at the Institute of Southeast Asian Studies.